llls

Books should be returned or renewed by the last date above. Renew by phone **08458 247 200** or online *www.kent.gov.uk/libs*

CUSTOMER SERVICE EXCELLENCE
UK
The Government Standard

Kent
County
Council

Libraries & Archives

C333660629

In This Book

QuickStart Guide

Your keys to understanding the city – we help you decide what to do and how to do it

Need to Know
Tips for a smooth trip

Neighborhoods
What's where

Explore Boston

The best things to see and do, neighborhood by neighborhood

Top Sights
Make the most of your visit

Local Life
The insider's city

The Best of Boston

The city's highlights in handy lists to help you plan

Best Walks
See the city on foot

Bostons' Best...
The best experiences

Survival Guide

Tips and tricks for a seamless, hassle-free city experience

Getting Around
Travel like a local

Essential Information
Including where to stay

Our selection of the city's best places to eat, drink and experience:

◉ **Sights**

✖ **Eating**

◻ **Drinking**

✪ **Entertainment**

🔒 **Shopping**

These symbols give you the vital information for each listing:

☑ Telephone Numbers	⛄ Family-Friendly
⊙ Opening Hours	🐾 Pet-Friendly
P Parking	⍰ Bus
⊖ Nonsmoking	⛴ Ferry
@ Internet Access	T Metro
🛜 Wi-Fi Access	S Subway
🍴 Vegetarian Selection	⍰ Tram
📖 English-Language Menu	⍰ Train

Find each listing quickly on maps for each neighbourhood:

Bar Hemingway

16   Map p233, B2

Legend has it that Hemi self, wielding a machine ...rate this timber-pan ...ered bar during ...en by Papa ar town. Dress ...s.com; Hôtel Rit ⊙6.30pm-2a

Lonely Planet's Boston

Lonely Planet Pocket Guides are designed to get you straight to the heart of the city.

Inside you'll find all the must-see sights, plus tips to make your visit to each one really memorable. We've split the city into easy-to-navigate neighborhoods and provided clear maps so you'll find your way around with ease. Our expert authors have searched out the best of the city: walks, food, nightlife and shopping, to name a few. Because you want to explore, our 'Local Life' pages will take you to some of the most exciting areas to experience the real Boston.

And of course you'll find all the practical tips you need for a smooth trip: itineraries for short visits, how to get around, and how much to tip the guy who serves you a drink at the end of a long day's exploration.

It's your guarantee of a really great experience.

Our Promise

You can trust our travel information because Lonely Planet authors visit the places we write about, each and every edition. We never accept freebies for positive coverage, so you can rely on us to tell it like it is.

QuickStart Guide

Welcome to Boston

Boston's winding streets recall revolution and renewal; even today, this is a forward-looking and barrier-breaking city. Though you can hardly walk a step without running into some historic site, Boston remains vital, with vibrant artistic scenes, cutting-edge urban planning, and ever-present scholars and thinkers shaping the evolving culture.

Crossing the Old Northern Avenue Bridge
LENA MIRISOLA/GETTY IMAGES ©

Boston
Top Sights

Trinity Church (p94)

With its elaborate sandstone exterior and mural-painted, stained-glass-lit interior, this centerpiece of Copley Square is the crowning achievement of architect Henry Hobson Richardson.

LOU JONES/GETTY IMAGES ©

Museum of Fine Arts (p110)

There's something for everybody at this encyclopedic art museum, but the highlight is the fantastic Art of the Americas wing, with special attention paid to Boston artists like Copley and Sargent.

Fenway Park (p114)

Fenway Park is the oldest baseball stadium in America, home to the beloved Boston Red Sox and site of countless heroics and heartbreaks in the past century.

Harvard Yard (p122)

The geographic and historic heart of Harvard University, this is the oldest part of the university, where red-brick buildings covered in green ivy exude academia.

New England Aquarium (p58)

After a renovation and expansion, the aquarium now boasts an outdoor marine mammal pavilion, a hands-on shark and ray touch-tank and a three-story ocean tank.

KIM GRANT/GETTY IMAGES ©

KINDRA CLINEFF/GETTY IMAGES ©

Boston Harbor Islands (p72)

This national park consists of 34 islands, many of which are open for trail walking, bird-watching, camping, kayaking and swimming.

Institute of Contemporary Art (p60)

The ICA has been at the forefront of the resurgent contemporary art scene in Boston; its dramatic building on the South Boston waterfront is a work of art in itself.

Isabella Stewart Gardner Museum (p112)

The magnificent Venetian-style palazzo is filled with thousands of paintings, tapestries and other treasures – a monument to one woman's taste for exquisite art.

Boston Public Library (p92)

On Copley Sq, the original building was inspired by a Renaissance palazzo. Through Daniel Chester French's bronze doorways, the library is filled with beautiful works.

Charlestown Navy Yard (p24)

Home to the storied USS *Constitution*, the Charlestown Navy Yard stands as an architectural and historical monument to the US Navy and its vessels.

Boston Common (p46)

The Boston Common is America's oldest public park and the start of the Freedom Trail (p136). Scattered with historical markers, it's a perfect stop for picnicking and people watching.

Boston Local Life

Insider tips to help you find the real city

It's no secret that Boston is rich in historic sites and cultural institutions; but it's also a city of dynamic neighborhoods and local people. Here's your introduction to the city's ethnic enclaves, student hangouts, local boutiques and art markets.

Italian Culture in the North End (p32)

▶ Irresistible food & drink
▶ Old-world ambiance

Wander the North End's warren of narrow streets to witness old-timers carrying on passionate discussions in Italian and playing *bocce* in the park, with stops to nosh at the *ristoranti* and *enoteche* (wine bars) that line the main streets.

South End Art Walk (p78)

▶ Local artists in their element
▶ Victorian architecture

Take a walk through the South End to hobnob with local artists and art dealers, admire the country's largest concentration of Victorian row houses and sample some of Boston's most innovative and exciting options for dining out.

Back Bay Fashion Walk (p96)

▶ Trendy boutiques
▶ Local design

A few local designers are part of Boston's burgeoning fashion scene, and they contribute to a uniquely wearable and wonderful sense of style. Take this stroll along Newbury St to see fashions created by Bostonians, for Bostonians.

Offbeat Harvard Square (p124)

▶ Bookstores & buskers
▶ Coffee shops

Cantabrigians rightly complain that Harvard Square has lost its edge, as shops once independently owned are gobbled up by national chains. But the square is still a vibrant place with an offbeat, artistic underbelly – you just have to know where to look.

Gelato in a North End bakery (p32)

Café Pamplona (p125), Harvard Square

Other great places to experience the city like a local:

Drinking in the North End (p42)

Hidden Beacon Hill (p53)

Downtown Lunch Break (p67)

Chinatown Market Tour (p82)

Charles River Esplanade (p104)

Food Trucks (p130)

Boston
Day Planner

Day One

Spend your first day in Boston following the **Freedom Trail**, which starts on the **Boston Common** (p46) and continues through Downtown. You won't have time to go inside every museum, but you can admire the architecture and learn the history. Highlights are the **Old South Meeting House** (p64), the **Old State House** (p64) and **Faneuil Hall** (p65). Grab lunch from one of the many outlets in **Quincy Market** (p136).

In the afternoon, the Freedom Trail continues into the North End, where you can visit the historic **Paul Revere House** (p36), **Old North Church** (p36) and **Copp's Hill Burying Ground** (p37). In Charlestown, tour the **USS Constitution** (p25) and climb the **Bunker Hill Monument** (p27).

For dinner, you are perfectly poised for an Italian feast along Hanover St, perhaps at **Pomodoro** (p39) or **Giacomo's Ristorante** (p39). Afterwards, head to the former Charles St Jail – now the exquisite Liberty Hotel – where you can sip cocktails under the soaring lobby or head down to the former 'drunk tank,' which now houses the ultracool club **Alibi** (p42).

Day Two

Spend the morning admiring Boston's most architecturally significant collection of buildings, clustered around Copley Sq. Inspect the art and books at the **Boston Public Library** (p92) and ogle the magnificent stained-glass windows at **Trinity Church** (p94). For lunch, treat yourself to some smart fine dining at the **Courtyard** (p100).

Your afternoon is reserved for one of Boston's magnificent art museums. Unfortunately, you'll have to choose between the excellent, encyclopedic collection of the **Museum of Fine Arts** (p110) and the smaller (but no less extraordinary) exhibits at the **Isabella Stewart Gardner Museum** (p112). Either way, you won't be disappointed.

In the evening, head to **Fenway Park** (p119) to see the Red Sox play baseball. If you're not lucky enough to score tickets, hang out at the **Bleacher Bar** (p118) to sneak a peek inside the ball park. If sports aren't your thing, you might prefer a performance by the world-class **Boston Symphony Orchestra** (p118), which takes place in the same neighborhood.

Short on time?
We've arranged Boston's must-sees into these day-by-day itineraries to make sure you see the very best of the city in the time you have available.

Day Three

Rent a bicycle from **Urban Adventours** (p37) and spend the morning cycling along the **Charles River Esplanade** (p104). Cross the river to Cambridge for scenic views of scullers and sailboats on the Charles, with the Boston city skyline as the backdrop.

While away the afternoon in **Harvard Sq** (p124), browsing the bookstores and cruising the cafes. Catch a free tour of **Harvard Yard** (p122).

Don't miss the chance to see whatever brilliant or bizarre production is playing at the **American Repertory Theater** (p131). If that doesn't take your fancy, go for drinks and live music at **Club Passim** (p131) or the **Sinclair** (p132).

Day Four

Spend the morning on the water, either on a **whale-watching tour** (p66) to Stellwagen Bank or a trip to the **Boston Harbor Islands** (p72). If the weather is not cooperating, get a closer view of the marine life inside the **New England Aquarium** (p58).

Afterwards, stroll along the HarborWalk and across the Old North Bridge, admiring the harbor views along the way. Have lunch with a view at **Sam's** (p67) or super-fresh seafood at **Yankee Lobster Co** (p67). Continue to the **Institute of Contemporary Art** (p60) for an afternoon of provocative contemporary art; don't miss the amazing view from the Founders' Gallery.

In the evening, explore the trend-setting South End. End your evening sipping cocktails and listening to jazz at the **Beehive** (p84).

Need to Know

For more information, see Survival Guide (p155)

Currency
US dollar ($)

Language
English

Visas
Citizens of many countries are eligible for the US Visa Waiver Program, which requires prior approval via the Electronic System for Travel Authorization (ESTA).

Money
ATMs widely available. Credit cards accepted at most hotels, restaurants and shops.

Cell Phones
Most US cell-phone systems are incompatible with the GSM 900/1800 standard used throughout Europe and Asia.

Time
Eastern Standard Time (GMT/UTC minus 5 hours)

Plugs & Adaptors
Plugs have two straight pins and a third (optional) round pin. Voltage is 120V. Travelers from Europe and the UK will require an adaptor and a transformer for some appliances.

Tipping
Tip at least 15% (more for good service) in all bars and restaurants.

❶ Before You Go

Your Daily Budget

Budget less than $80
▶ Dorm bed $30–$50

▶ Cheap eats in Chinatown and self-catering

▶ Take advantage of free museum nights and walking tours

Midrange $150–$300
▶ Double room in a midrange hotel $125–$250

▶ Two-course dinner $20–$30

▶ Buy joint museum tickets, tour add-ons and discounted theater tickets

Top End more than $300
▶ Double room in a top-end hotel from $250

▶ Two-course dinner with wine from $50

▶ Enjoy a range of concerts, events and activities

Useful Websites

Lonely Planet (www.lonelyplanet.com/boston) Destination information, hotel bookings, traveler forum and more.

Boston.com (www.boston.com) Event listings, restaurant reviews, local news and more.

My Secret Boston (www.mysecretboston.com) The best secrets even locals don't know.

Advance Planning

One month before Reserve a place to stay, especially for budget travel and in late spring or fall.

Two weeks before Buy tickets for the Boston Symphony Orchestra or the Red Sox.

One week before Make your dinner reservations.

2 Arriving in Boston

Most visitors will arrive at Logan International Airport or, by train, at South Station. Both are easily accessible by metro trains, better known as 'the T,' operated by the MBTA (see right).

✈ From Logan

Destination	Best Transport
Back Bay	Blue line to green line T
Beacon Hill	Silver line bus to red line T
Cambridge	Silver line bus to red line T
Chinatown	Silver line bus
Downtown & Waterfront	Silver line bus
Kenmore Sq & Fenway	Blue line to green line T
West End	Blue line to green or orange line T

🚋 From South Station

Destination	Best Transport
Back Bay	Red line to green line T
Beacon Hill	Red line T
Cambridge	Red line T
Chinatown	Walk
Downtown & Waterfront	Walk
Kenmore Sq & Fenway	Red line to green line T
West End	Red line to green or orange line T

At the Airport

Logan International Airport Has all the facilities you would expect. Its five terminals are connected by the frequent shuttle bus 11. Downtown Boston, just a few miles away, is accessible by metro (the T), bus, water shuttle and taxi.

3 Getting Around

Boston is a wonderful walking or cycling city. Otherwise, most of the main attractions are accessible by metro (subway). Bus and metro fares are slightly cheaper if you use a plastic 'Charlie Card', which is available at any station.

T Metro (the T)

The **MBTA** (☎800-392-6100, 617-222-3200; www.mbta.com; per ride $2-2.50; ⏰5:30am-12:30am Sun-Thu, to 2am Fri & Sat) operates the USA's oldest subway, known locally as 'the T,' which will take you almost anywhere you want to go in Boston.

🚌 Bus

The MBTA operates many bus routes within the city. The silver line is a 'rapid' bus that is useful for Logan Airport (SL1) and the South End (SL5)

🚲 Bicycle (Hubway)

Boston's bike-share program is the **Hubway** (www.thehubway.com; 30min free, 60/90/120min $2/6/14; ⏰24hr). There are hundreds of bikes that are available for short-term loan at Hubway stations all around town. Purchase a temporary membership at any bicycle kiosk, then pay by the half hour to use the bikes. Return the bike to any station in the vicinity of your destination.

Boston
Neighborhoods

Back Bay (p90)
Boston's most prestigious address, boasting grand Victorian architecture and high-end fashion boutiques.

⊙ Top Sights

Boston Public Library

Trinity Church

Harvard Yard ⊙

Cambridge (p120)
A separate city and home of Harvard University. Art, history and eating options to rival its counterpart across the river.

⊙ Top Sights

Harvard Yard

Kenmore Square & Fenway (p108)
Home to institutions including the Museum of Fine Arts, the Boston Symphony Orchestra and Fenway Park.

⊙ Top Sights

Museum of Fine Arts

Isabella Stewart Gardner Museum

Fenway Park

Fenway ⊙ Park

Isabella Stewart Gardner Museum ⊙ ⊙ Museum of Fine Arts

Worth a Trip (p72)
⊙ Top Sights

Boston Harbor Islands

Beacon Hill & Boston Common (p44)

Antique shops and iconic architecture characterize this quintessential Boston neighborhood.

◉ **Top Sights**

Boston Common

Charlestown (p22)

A historic neighborhood filled with colonial architecture and war memorials.

◉ **Top Sights**

Charlestown Navy Yard

West End & North End (p30)

Among the oldest parts of the city, now home to a lively Italian immigrant population.

Charlestown Navy Yard ◉

New England Aquarium ◉

Boston Common ◉

◉ *Trinity Church*

◉ *Boston Public Library*

◉ *Institute of Contemporary Art*

South End & Chinatown (p76)

Overlapping districts offering authentic Asian food, sparkling theater marquees, cutting-edge art galleries and top-notch dining.

Downtown & Waterfront (p56)

The hub of tourist activity, with historic sites, waterside walks and sightseeing boats.

◉ **Top Sights**

New England Aquarium

Institute of Contemporary Art

Explore
Boston

Worth a Trip

Boston Harbor and city skyline
GARETH MCCORMACK/GETTY IMAGES ©

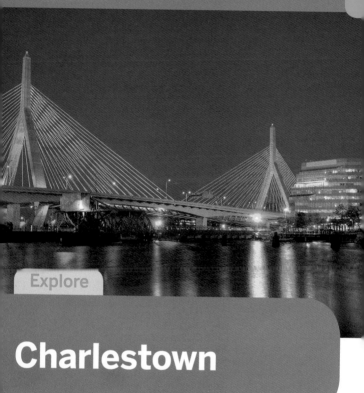

Explore

Charlestown

The site of the original settlement of the Massachusetts Bay Colony, Charlestown is the terminus of the Freedom Trail. Many tourists tramp across these historic cobblestone sidewalks to admire the USS *Constitution* and climb to the top of the Bunker Hill Monument, which towers above the neighborhood.

The Sights in a Day

☼ Walk across the Charlestown Bridge from North Station, or catch the ferry from Long Wharf, to arrive at the Charlestown waterfront. Your first stop is the **Charlestown Navy Yard** (p24), including a film at the visitor center, a tour of the **USS Constitution** (p25) and a few hours investigating the **USS Constitution Museum** (p25). Take a detour from the Freedom Trail to have lunch at **Pier Six** (p29), with amazing views of the Boston Harbor and city skyline.

☼ After lunch, stroll inland to explore the neighborhood's aged narrow streets, lined with 19th-century Federal and colonial houses, and make your way to the **Bunker Hill Monument** (p27). Get a history lesson at the **Bunker Hill Museum** (p27), then climb to the top of the obelisk for panoramic views.

☾ In the evening, make a reservation for dinner at the delightful **Navy Yard Bistro & Wine Bar** (p28).

 Top Sights

Charlestown Navy Yard (p24)

♥ **Best of Boston**

Drinking

Warren Tavern (p29)

Pier Six (p29)

For Kids

USS Constitution Museum (p25)

For Free

Charlestown Navy Yard (p24)

Bunker Hill Monument (p27)

Getting There

⚓ **Boat** The F4 ferry (p158) runs every 15 to 30 minutes between Pier 3 in Charlestown and Long Wharf on the Boston waterfront.

🚌 **Bus** Bus 93 runs between Haymarket and Charlestown every 20 minutes.

🇹 **Metro** The closest T-stations are Community College station (orange line) and North Station (orange and green lines), both a 20-minute walk from the Charlestown sights.

Top Sights
Charlestown Navy Yard

No longer operational, the Charlestown Navy Yard stands as an architectural and historical monument to the US Navy and its vessels. The oldest commissioned US Navy ship, the USS *Constitution*, has been moored here since 1897. Another formidable warship, the USS *Cassin Young*, is also docked here, inviting visitors to learn about its feats during WWII. There is an excellent museum dedicated to the USS *Constitution* and more general naval history, while the rest of the shipyard remembers the history of the shipbuilding industry.

👁 Map p26, C3

www.nps.gov/bost

admission free

🕑 9am-5pm

🚌 93 from Haymarket,
🚢 F4 from Long Wharf,
Ⓣ North Station

Don't Miss

USS *Constitution*

'Her sides are made of iron!' cried a crewman as he watched a shot bounce off the thick oak hull of the **USS Constitution** (www.oldironsides. com; Charlestown Navy Yard; admission free; ⏰10am-6pm Tue-Sun Apr-Oct, to 4pm Thu-Sun Nov-Mar) during the War of 1812 – thus earning the legendary ship her nickname, 'Old Ironsides.' Indeed, the ship has never gone down in a battle, and is still the oldest commissioned US Navy vessel, dating from 1797.

USS Constitution Museum

For a play-by-play account of the various battles of the USS *Constitution,* head to the **USS Constitution Museum** (www.ussconstitutionmuseum.org; First Ave, Charlestown Navy Yard; donation adult/senior/child $5/3/2; ⏰9am-6pm Apr-Oct, 10am-5pm Nov-Mar). The exhibit on the Barbary War explains the birth of the US Navy during this relatively unknown conflict – America's first war at sea. Upstairs, kids can experience what it is like to be a sailor on the USS *Constitution* in 1812.

USS *Cassin Young*

A formidable example of a Fletcher-class destroyer – a WWII craft that was the Navy's fastest, most versatile ship at the time – **USS Cassin Young** (admission free; ⏰10am-4pm Tue-Sun Apr-Jun & Sep-Nov, to 5pm Jul-Aug) participated in the 1944 Battle of Leyte Gulf, as well as the 1945 invasion of Okinawa. Here, the ship sustained two kamikaze hits, leaving 23 crew members dead and many more wounded. Take a free, 45-minute tour, or wander around the main deck on your own.

☑ **Top Tips**

▶ A free, 10-minute introductory film about the Charlestown Navy Yard is shown throughout the day at the **NPS Visitors Center** (☎617-242-5601; www.nps.gov/bost; ⏰9am-5pm Apr-Jun & Oct-Nov, 9am-6pm Jul-Sep, closed Mon Dec-Mar; Ⓣ North Station).

▶ All visitors over the age of 18 must show a photo ID to board the USS *Constitution*.

▶ Navy personnel give guided tours of the ship's top deck, gun deck and cramped quarters (last tour 5:30pm in summer, 3:30pm in winter). You can also wander around the top deck by yourself, but access is limited.

✗ **Take a Break**

Stroll northeast along the waterfront for lunch with a view at **Pier Six** (p29). There are also a few restaurants and cafes (including an ice cream place) at City Sq, a half mile southwest of the Navy Yard.

Pier 8

Pier 7

Pier 6

8

9

Pier 5

Thirteenth St

First Ave

Ninth St

Fourth Ave

Eighth St

Shipyard Park

Boston Inner Harbor

Sixth St

4

Third Ave

MBTA Inner Harbor Ferry (F4)

Pier 3

Pier 2

Fifth St

Pier 1

NORTH END

Decatur St

Second Ave

MBTA Water Shuttle

MBTA Water Shuttle

MBTA Water Shuttle

CHARLESTOWN

Chelsea St

Lowney St

Bunker Hill St

Tremont St

Prospect St

Charlestown Navy Yard

Lexington St

Mt Vernon Ave

Mt Vernon St

Adams St

Chestnut St

Northern Expwy

Constitution Rd

Putnam St

Winthrop Square

Park St

Monument Square

1

Bunker Hill Museum

2

Winthrop St

Soley St

N Washington S

Barratt St

Monument

Mt Vernon St

Monument Ave

Pleasant St

Cordis St

Main St

City Square

Great House Site

3

Charles River

Cross St

Green St

High St

Warren St

6

7

Harvard St

Rutherford Ave

Paul Revere Park

Elm St

Wood St

Union St

Devens St

Prescott St

Zakim Bridg

Rutherford Ave

93

1

For reviews see	
◉ Top Sights	p24
◉ Sights	p27
✗ Eating	p28
◑ Drinking	p29

200 m

0.1 miles

N

Bunker Hill Monument

Sights

Bunker Hill Monument   MONUMENT

1 ◉ Map p26, B1

This 220ft granite obelisk monument commemorates the bloody battle on June 17, 1775 (see p28). Climb the 294 steps to the top of the monument to enjoy the panorama of the city, the harbor and the North Shore.
(www.nps.gov/bost; Monument Sq; admission free; ☺9am-5pm Sep-Jun, to 6pm Jul & Aug; 🚍93 from Haymarket, T Community College)

Bunker Hill Museum   MUSEUM

2 ◉ Map p26, B2

Opposite the Bunker Hill Monument, this red-brick museum contains two floors of exhibits, including historical dioramas, a few artifacts and an impressive, 360-degree mural depicting the battle. If you can find where the artist signed his masterpiece, you win a prize.
(43 Monument Sq; admission free; ☺9am-5pm; 🚍93 from Haymarket, T Community College)

Great House Site   ARCHAEOLOGICAL SITE

3 ◉ Map p26, B3

Besides being an urban plaza, the City Square is also an archaeological site.

The Big Dig construction project un-earthed the foundation of a structure called the Great House, widely believed to be the house of Massachusetts Bay Colony Governor John Winthrop and the seat of government in 1630. (City Sq; admission free; ⏰dawn-dusk; 🚢F4 from Long Wharf, Ⓣ North Station)

Eating

Navy Yard Bistro & Wine Bar
FRENCH $$

4 🍴 Map p26, D2

Dark and romantic, this hideaway is tucked into an unlikely spot facing a pedestrian walkway, allowing for comfortable outdoor seating in summer months. Inside, the cozy, carved-wood interior is an ideal date destination – perfect for tuna tartare or brined pork chops.

(www.navyyardbistro.com; cnr Second Ave & Sixth St; mains $17-26; ⏰5-10pm; 🚌93 from Haymarket, 🚢F4 from Long Wharf)

Figs
ITALIAN $$

5 🍴 Map p26, B2

This creative pizzeria – which also has an outlet in **Beacon Hill** (42 Charles St; mains $15-20; ⏰11:30am-10pm; 🚶; Ⓣ Charles/MGH) – is the brainchild of celebrity chef Todd English, who tops whisper-thin crusts with interest-ing, exotic toppings. Case in point: the namesake fig and prosciutto with gorgonzola cheese. The menu also includes sandwiches and fresh pasta. While the food tastes gourmet, the dining room is dark, comfy and casual

(www.toddenglishfigs.com; 67 Main St; mains $15-20; ⏰11:30am-10pm; 🚶🚼; Ⓣ Community College)

Understand
The Battle of Bunker Hill

- - - - - - - - - - - - - - - - - -

'Don't fire until you see the whites of their eyes!' came the order from Colonel Prescott to revolutionary troops on June 17, 1775, as they assem-bled on Breed's Hill. Considering the ill-preparedness of the ragtag colonial soldiers, the bloody battle that followed resulted in a surprising number of British casualties. Ultimately, the Redcoats prevailed, but the victory was bittersweet. They lost more than one-third of their deployed forces, while the colonists suffered relatively few casualties. Equally importantly, the battle demonstrated the gumption of the upstart revolutionaries.

The revolutionaries' biggest loss was General Joseph Warren, who was fighting on the front line and was killed by a musket shot to the head in the final British charge. A few weeks later, George Washington assumed com-mand of the ragged Continental Army on the Cambridge Common.

Top Tip
Climbing Bunker Hill
From April to June, you must obtain a climbing pass before ascending the Bunker Hill Monument. Passes are available on a first-come-first-serve basis from the Bunker Hill Museum (p27).

Tangierino

MOROCCAN $$$

6 🍴 Map p26, A2

This unexpected gem transports guests from a colonial town house to a sultan's palace. The North African specialties include *harira* (a traditional tomato and lentil soup), couscous and tajine, all with a modern flair. The highlight is the sexy interior, complete with thick carpets, plush pillows and jewel-toned tapestries. Belly dancers may or may not enhance the atmosphere.

(📞617-242-6009; www.tangierino.com; 83 Main St; mains $25-40; ⏱5pm-1am; 🚇Community College)

Drinking

Warren Tavern

HISTORIC PUB

7 🍺 Map p26, A2

One of the oldest pubs in Boston, the Warren Tavern has been pouring pints for its customers since George Washington and Paul Revere drank here. It is named for General Joseph Warren, a fallen hero of the Battle of Bunker Hill (shortly after which – in 1780 – this pub was opened). (www.warrentavern.com; 2 Pleasant St; ⏱11am-1am Mon-Fri, 10am-1am Sat & Sun; 🚇Community College)

Pier Six

BAR

8 🍺 Map p26, E3

This revamped waterfront restaurant offers a spectacular panorama of the Boston Harbor and city skyline, with floor-to-ceiling windows and a large outdoor deck for your optimal viewing pleasure. The food is not particularly noteworthy, but there are several types of oyster on the half shell to accompany the excellent selection of craft beers.

(www.pier6boston.com; 1 8th St, Pier 6; ⏱11:30am-11:30pm, later in summer; 🚌93 from Haymarket, 🚢F4 from Long Wharf, 🚇North Station)

 Local Life
Zume's Coffee House
Locals love **Zume's** (off Map p26, A1; www.zumescoffeehouse.com; 223 Main St; ⏱6am-6pm Mon-Fri, 7am-6pm Sat & Sun; 📶♿; 🚇Community College) – pronounced Zoomies – for the comfy leather chairs, big cups of coffee and decadent doughnuts. Also on the menu: soup, sandwiches and lunchy items. Paintings and photographs by local artists adorn the walls; books and games keep the kiddies busy.

Explore

West End & North End

Although the West End and North End are physically adjacent, at-mospherically they're worlds apart. The West End is an institutional area without much zest. By contrast, the North End is delightfully spicy, thanks to the many Italian *ristoranti* and *salumerie* (delis) that line the streets. The Freedom Trail also winds through here, passing by landmarks that date to the 17th century.

The Sights in a Day

☼ Spend the morning gawking at dinosaur bones, spying on butterflies, programming robots and investigating alternative energy, all at the **Museum of Science** (p36). For lunch, stroll into the North End for pizza from **Galleria Umberto** (p39) or shellfish from **Neptune Oyster** (p39).

☼ Now you are perfectly placed to spend your afternoon exploring the North End. Visit the **Paul Revere House** (p36) at North Sq, then stroll and shop along Hanover St. Traverse the Paul Revere Mall to arrive at **Old North Church** (p36), and continue on to **Copp's Hill Burying Ground** (p37).

☾ Pick a North End establishment for dinner and treat yourself to an Italian feast. Afterwards, have a drink at **Caffe Vittoria** (p41) or catch a show at **Improv Asylum** (p42).

For a local's day in the North End, see p32.

○ Local Life

Italian Culture in the North End (p32)

♥ Best of Boston

Eating

Pomodoro (p39)

Neptune Oyster (p39)

Maria's Pastry (p32)

Galleria Umberto (p39)

Pizzeria Regina (p40)

Drinking

Ward 8 (p41)

Boston Beer Works (p42)

Caffé dello Sport (p42)

Entertainment

Improv Asylum (p42)

Shopping

Twilight (p43)

Getting There

Ⓣ **Metro** At the junction of the green and orange lines, North Station is convenient for the West End.

Ⓣ **Metro** For the North End, the closest T-station is Haymarket, which lies on both the green and the orange lines.

Local Life
Italian Culture in the North End

The North End's warren of alleyways retains the old-world flavor brought by Italian immigrants, ever since they started settling here in the early 20th century. And when we say 'flavor', we're not being metaphorical. We mean garlic, basil and oregano, sauteed in extra virgin olive oil; rich tomato sauces that have simmered for hours; amaretto and anise; and cold, creamy gelato.

....

1 North End Park
Grab a snack of fresh cheese and olives from **J Pace & Son** (www.jpaceandson.com; 42 Cross St; mains $8-12; ⊙9am-7pm; 🖋; T Haymarket) or cannoli from **Maria's Pastry** (www.mariaspastry.com; 46 Cross St; ⊙7am-7pm Mon-Sat, to 5pm Sun; 🖋; T Haymarket), then cross the street to sit in shade under grape vines

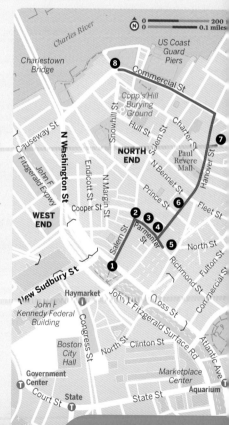

in North End Park, designed as the neighborhood's 'front porch.'

2 Polcari's Coffee

Since 1932, **Polcari's Coffee** (www.polcariscoffee.com; 105 Salem St; ⊙9:30am-6pm Mon-Sat; ⊤Haymarket) is where North Enders stock up on their beans. Look for 27 kinds of imported coffee, over 150 spices and an impressive selection of legumes, grains and loose teas.

3 North End Branch Library

The **local library** (25 Parmenter St; ⊙10am-6pm Mon-Sat; ⊤Haymarket) contains an impressive plaster model of the Palazzo Ducale in Venice, built in the early 20th century by a local artist and school teacher, Miss Henrietta Macy, who moved to Venice but never forgot her students back in Boston. Figurines of 16th-century Venetians show off the fashions of the era.

4 Gigi Gelateria

Gelato is a denser, softer version of American ice cream. It's made with milk instead of cream, giving it a lower fat content, but it's no less satisfying on a hot day – stop by **Gigi Gelateria** (www.gelateriacorp.com; 272 Hanover St; gelato $3-5; ⊙10am-midnight; ⊤Haymarket) to sample one of their dozens of flavors.

5 Salumeria Italiana

Shelves stocked with extra-virgin olive oil and aged balsamic vinegar; cases crammed with cured meats, hard cheeses and olives of all shapes and sizes; boxes of pasta; jars of sauce – the **Salumeria Italiana** (www.salumeriaitaliana. com; 151 Richmond St; ⊙7am-6pm Mon-Thu, to 7pm Fri & Sat; ⊤Haymarket) is the archetype of North End specialty shops.

6 St Leonard's Church

Founded in 1873, **St Leonard's** (www.saintleonardchurchboston.org; 320 Hanover St; ⊙9:30am-2:30pm) is the first church in New England built by Italian immigrants. If the church is open, peek inside to see the city's oldest shrine to St Anthony, most beloved of Italian saints. The attached Peace Garden is always open for a sacred moment of serenity.

7 All Saints' Way

'Mock all and sundry things, but leave the saints alone' – so goes an old Italian saying posted on the wall of this tiny **alleyway** (4 Battery St; ⊤Haymarket) and surrounded by thousands of images of saints. The shrine is the pet project of local resident Peter Baldassari, who has been collecting holy cards since his childhood.

8 Langone Park

Designed by Frederick Law Olmsted, this peaceful waterside **park** (Commercial St; ⊤North Station) belies the history of this site: in 1919, a huge distillery tank burst, sending forth a flood of molasses that destroyed homes, killed 21 people and injured hundreds more. Nowadays, you'll see North Enders speaking Italian and playing bocce. Take in the harbor views and enjoy!

A　B　C　D

🧭 N　0 _____ 400 m
0 _____ 0.2 miles

1

● 1
Museum of
Science

Charles River

Suffolk
County
Jail

Beverly St

Zakim Bridge

🅣 Science
Park

Nashua St
Charles St
Martha Rd

☆ 20
TD Garden

North 🅡 🅣
Station

2

Storrow Dr

WEST END

O'Neill
Federal
Building

Lomasney Way

Causeway St

17 🅣

Friend St

Portland St

The
Esplanade

Blossom St

Massachusetts
General Hospital

Shriner's
Burn
Institute

William Cardinal O'Connell Way

Staniford St

Merrimac St

New
Chardon St
Courthouse

3

Fruit St

Parkman St

Blossom St

State
Service
Center

New Chardon St

Hawkins St

4

🅟
18

Cambridge St

● Bowdoin
🅣

🅣
Charles/MGH

Grove St

Anderson St

Garden St

Irving St

Russell St

Joy St

Hancock St

Ridgeway La

Temple St

Bowdoin St

Saltonstall
Building

Somerset St

Cente
Plaza

Court
House

Phillips St

Revere St

Myrtle St

**BEACON
HILL**

Derne St

Ashburton Pl

Suffolk
County Court
House

Pinckney St

5

For reviews see	
⊙ Sights	p36
✕ Eating	p37
✕ Drinking	p41
☆ Entertainment	p42
🔒 Shopping	p42

E

Charlestown Bridge

Lovejoy Pl

Commercial St

F

Snowhill St

North End
Playground

Foster St

G

US Coast
Guard
Piers

Hanover St

H

Constitution
Wharf

1

Copp's Hill
Terrace

4
Copp's
Hill Burying
Ground

Henchman St

NORTH
END

Defilippo
Playground

Hull St

Sheate St

Old
North
Church

3

Unity St

Charter St

Battery St

21

Salutation St

Medford St

Haverhill St

15

Thatcher St

14

Prince St

Salem St

N Bennet St

Tileston St

Paul
Revere
Mall

Hanover Ave

Harris St

North St

Clark St

Sumner Tunnel (toll)

2

Callahan Tunnel

Lynn St

N Margin St

Cooper St

Valenti Way

Canal St

Endicott St

Morton St

Wiget St

Parmenter St

23

16

11

10

9

6

7

2

12

Moon St

Fleet St

Lewis St

North
Square
Paul
Revere
House

Commercial St

Atlantic Ave

3

25

13

8

19

Salem St

Hanover St

24

North St

Richmond St

Fulton St

Mercantile
Wharf Building

North
End Park

New Sudbury St

Haymarket

John F Kennedy
Federal Building

Congress St

Union St

Creek Sq

Blackstone St

John F Fitzgerald Surface Rd

Cross St

North St

Clinton St

Commercial St

Urban
AdvenTours

5

Christopher
Columbus
Park

WATERFRONT

4

Cambridge St

City Hall
Plaza

Boston
City
Hall

Dock
Square

North St

John F Fitzgerald Expwy

Aquarium

5

Government
Center

Court St

State

DOWNTOWN

State St

Chatham St

India St

Purchase St

Central St

Sights

Museum of Science
MUSEUM

1 Map p34, A1

This educational playground has more than 600 interactive exhibits. The impressive array of exhibits explores computers, technology, complex systems, algae, maps, models, dinosaurs and birds. Many others focus on the natural world, including exploration of issues such as organic waste as an alternative fuel source, pathogens on produce and climate change. (www.mos.org; Charles River Dam; adult/child/senior $23/20/21, theater & planetarium $10/8/9; ⏱9am-5pm Sat-Thu Sep-Jun, to 7pm Jul & Aug, to 9pm Fri year-round; P♿; TScience Park)

Paul Revere House
HISTORIC HOUSE

2 Map p34, G3

When silversmith Paul Revere rode to warn patriots of the British march to Concord, he set out from his home on North Square. This small clapboard house, built in 1680, is the oldest house in Boston. A self-guided tour gives a glimpse of what life was like for the family – which included 16 children! (www.paulreverehouse.org; 19 North Sq; adult/child/senior & student $3.50/1/3; ⏱9:30am-5:15pm mid-Apr–Oct, to 4:15pm Nov–mid-Apr, closed Mon Jan-Mar; ♿; THaymarket)

Old North Church
CHURCH

3 Map p34, G2

It was here, on the night of April 18, 1775, that the sexton hung two lanterns from the steeple, as a signal that the British would march on Lexington and Concord via the sea route. Also called Christ Church, this 1723 place of worship is Boston's oldest church, featuring original brass chandeliers and bells dating to 1744 in the steeple. (www.oldnorth.com; 193 Salem St; requested donation $3, tour adult/child $6/4; ⏱9am-5pm Mar-Oct, 10am-4pm Tue-Sun Nov-Feb; THaymarket or North Station)

Understand

West End Museum

The West End, formerly a vibrant ethnic neighborhood, was razed by 'urban renewal' in the 1950s. Now it's dominated by concrete monoliths and institutional buildings. The **West End Museum** (Map p34, C3; www.thewestendmuseum.org; 150 Staniford St; admission free; ⏱11am-5pm Tue-Fri, to 4pm Sat; TNorth Station) is dedicated to preserving the memory of this neighborhood and educating the public about the ramifications of unchecked urban development. *The Last Tenement* exhibit traces the neighborhood's history from 1850 to 1958, highlighting its immigrant populations, economic evolution and eventual destruction.

STEVE LEWIS/GETTY IMAGES ©

Old North Church interior

Copp's Hill Burying Ground

CEMETERY

4 🎯 Map p34, F1

The city's second-oldest cemetery – dating to 1660 – is the final resting place for an estimated 10,000 souls. It is named for William Copp, who originally owned this land. While the oldest graves belong to Copp's children, there are several other noteworthy residents, including the austere Mather family. (Hull St; ⊙dawn-dusk; T North Station)

Urban AdvenTours

BICYCLE TOUR

5 🎯 Map p34, G4

Founded by avid cyclists who believe the best views of Boston are from a bicycle. The City View Ride provides a great overview of getting around by bike, but there are other specialty tours such as Bikes at Night and Bike & Brew Tour. They also rent bikes and helmets if you wish to cycle the city independently. (☎617-379-3590; www.urbanadventours.com; 103 Atlantic Ave; tours $50; 🚲; T Aquarium)

Eating

Volle Nolle

FUSION $$

6 🍴 Map p34, G3

Apparently, *volle nolle* is Latin for 'willy nilly,' but there's nothing haphazard about this much-beloved restaurant. Black-slate tables and pressed-tin walls

Understand

Revolutionary Boston

Called the Birthplace of the American Revolution, Boston played an incendiary role in the colonies' fight for independence.

No Taxation Without Representation

In the 1760s, the British Parliament passed a series of acts that placed greater financial burdens on the colonists. With each new tax, resentment in Boston intensified, as did vocal protests and violent mobs; respected local lawyer John Adams cited the Magna Carta's principle of 'no taxation without representation.' To each act of rebellion, the British throne responded with increasingly severe measures, eventually dispatching Redcoats to restore order and suspending all local political power in Boston.

Sons of Liberty

Unrepentant Bostonians went underground. The Sons of Liberty, a clandestine network of patriots, stirred up public resistance to British policy and harassed the king's loyalists. Led by some well-known townsmen, including surgeon Dr Joseph Warren, merchant John Hancock, silversmith Paul Revere and brewer Sam Adams, they organized acts of protest, instigating the Boston Massacre and advocating for the Boston Tea Party.

After the Tea Party, the port was blockaded and Boston placed under military rule. The Sons of Liberty spread news of this latest outrage down the seaboard. The cause of Boston was becoming the cause of all the colonies – American Independence versus British Tyranny.

The Shot Heard Around the World

In April 1775 British General Gage dispatched troops to arrest fugitives Sam Adams and John Hancock and to seize a hidden stash of gunpowder. Informants tipped off Joseph Warren, who passed word to the Old North Church sexton to hang two lanterns in the steeple – a signal to Paul Revere, who slipped across the river to Charlestown, mounted his horse and galloped into the night to alert the local militia, the Minutemen.

At daybreak, the confrontation occurred. British soldiers skirmished with the Minutemen on the Old North Bridge in Concord and on the Lexington Green. By midmorning, more militia had arrived and the Redcoats were chased back to Boston in ignominious defeat. The inevitable had arrived: the War for Independence.

adorn the simple, small space. The nightly changing menu is also short but stellar – look for innovations such as duck meatballs, spicy chickpeas with chorizo, or pappardelle with foraged mushrooms. Cash only.

(351 Hanover St; mains $15-24; ⊙5:30-10pm Tue-Sun; 🖊️🚼; Ⓣ Haymarket)

Pomodoro ITALIAN $$$

7 Map p34, G3

This hole-in-the-wall place on Hanover is one of the North End's most romantic settings for delectable Italian. The food is simply but perfectly prepared: fresh pasta, spicy tomato sauce, grilled fish and meats, and wine by the glass. Credit cards are not accepted and the bathroom is smaller than your closet, but that's all part of the charm.

(📞617-367-4348; 319 Hanover St; brunch mains $12, dinner mains $23-24; ⊙5-11pm Mon-Fri, noon-11pm Sat & Sun; Ⓣ Haymarket)

Neptune Oyster SEAFOOD $$$

8 Map p34, F3

The menu hints at Italian, but you'll also find elements of Mexican, French and old-fashioned New England. The daily seafood specials and impressive raw bar (featuring several kinds of oysters, plus littlenecks, cherrystones, crabs and mussels) confirm that this is not your traditional North End eatery.

(📞617-742-3474; www.neptuneoyster.com; 63 Salem St; mains $19-35; ⊙11:30am-10pm, to 11pm Fri & Sat; Ⓣ Haymarket)

Giacomo's Ristorante ITALIAN $$

9 Map p34, G3

Customers line up before the doors open so they can guarantee a spot in the first round of seating at this old-school North End favorite. Enthusiastic and entertaining waiters, plus cramped quarters, ensure that you get to know your neighbors. The cuisine is no-frills southern Italian fare, served in unbelievable portions. Cash only.

(www.giacomosblog-boston.blogspot.com; 355 Hanover St; mains $14-19; ⊙4:30-10pm Mon-Sat, 4-9:30pm Sun; 🖊️; Ⓣ Haymarket)

Galleria Umberto PIZZA $$

10 Map p34, G3

Paper plates, cans of soda, Sicilian pizza: can't beat it. This lunchtime legend closes as soon as the slices are gone – and considering their thick and chewy goodness, that's often before the official 2:30pm closing time. Loyal patrons line up early so they are sure to get theirs. Slices are only $1.65, so don't bother with the credit card.

(289 Hanover St; mains $2-6; ⊙11am-2:30pm Mon-Sat; 🖊️🚼; Ⓣ Haymarket)

Carmelina's ITALIAN $$

11 Map p34, G3

Carmelina's offers a contemporary take on Italian hospitality, with large windows opening onto the street and bar stools facing the open kitchen. But the fare is tried-and-true traditional, with favorites being Mimmo's Baked

Meatballs and Sunday Macaroni (served every day of the week). (www.carmelinasboston.com; 307 Hanover St; mains $16-24; ⏱noon-10:30pm; ⚲; Ⓣ Haymarket)

Carmen   ITALIAN $$$

12 Map p34, G3

Exposed brick walls and candlelit tables are good for romance; interesting and exotic menu combinations are good for culinary indulgence. The innovative menu offers a selection of small plates providing a fresh take on traditional fare; mains such as pan-seared duck breast and roasted rack of pork sit alongside classic pasta dishes. (⚲617-742-6421; www.carmenboston.com; 33 North Sq, lunch mains $14-21, dinner mains $23-36; ⏱noon-3pm Thu-Sat, 5:30-9pm Tue-Sun; Ⓣ Haymarket)

Pauli's   SANDWICHES $

13 Map p34, F3

If you're in the mood for a 'lobsta roll,' head directly to Pauli's and he'll serve up 7oz of pink succulent goodness stuffed into a lightly grilled hot dog roll, just the way it's meant to be. The menu of sandwiches is extensive and most are tasty. The California Wrap is popular among the health-conscious. (www.paulisnorthend.com; 65 Salem St; sandwiches $7-9, lobster roll $16; ⏱8am-9pm Mon-Sat, 9am-5pm Sun; 📶; Ⓣ Haymarket)

Pizzeria Regina   PIZZA $

14 Map p34, F2

The queen of North End pizzerias is the legendary Pizzeria Regina, famous for brusque but endearing waitresses and crispy, thin-crust pizza. Thanks to the slightly spicy sauce (flavored with aged romano) Regina repeatedly wins

---

Understand
Ward 8

Back in the day, Ward 8 was the political division that encompassed the West End – the territory of local politician and 'ward boss' Martin Lomasney. Also known as 'the Mahatma,' Lomasney was a key player in the Democratic party machine, adept at trading in political favors and patronage.

His long political legacy includes the quintessential Boston cocktail, the Ward 8. As the story goes, Lomasney gathered with his supporters on the eve of his election to the state legislature. His victory was a foregone conclusion, so the bartender at the venerable Locke-Ober restaurant created a new drink to celebrate. The resulting cocktail, essentially a whiskey sour with a dash of grenadine, was named for the district that would swing the election.

Ironically, Lomasney was a Prohibitionist, and after his election this cocktail and others were outlawed. That's not doing anyone any favors, Mr Lomasney.

DAVID MCGLYNN/GETTY IMAGES ©

Coffee, Boston diner

accolades for her pies. Reservations are not accepted, so be prepared to wait. (www.pizzeriaregina.com; 11½ Thatcher St; pizzas $14-20; ☺11am-11:30pm; ✈; ⓉHaymarket)

Drinking

Ward 8
COCKTAIL BAR

15 🚇 Map p34, E2

The bartenders at this throwback know their stuff, mixing up a slew of specialty cocktails (including the namesake Ward 8) and serving them in clever thematic containers. The menu also features craft beers and tempting New American cuisine (try the duck wings). The atmosphere is classy but convivial – an excellent addition to the North/West End scene. There's brunch on weekends. (www.ward8.com; 90 N Washington St; ☺5-11pm; ⓉNorth Station)

Caffè Vittoria
CAFE

16 🚇 Map p34, G3

A delightful destination for dessert or aperitifs. The frilly parlor displays antique espresso machines and black-and-white photos, with a pressed-tin ceiling reminiscent of the era. Grab a marble-topped table, order a cappuccino and live it up in Victorian pleasure. Cash only, just like the olden days. (www.vittoriacaffe.com; 290-96 Hanover St; ☺7am-midnight; ⓉHaymarket)

Boston Beer Works

BREWERY

17 Map p34, D2

This is a solid option for lovers of beer and sports (and conveniently located near Boston's major sporting venues). The excellent selection of microbrews offers something for everyone, including plenty of seasonal specialties. Fruity brews (like blueberry ale) get rave reviews, with tasty sweet-potato fries as the perfect accompaniment. A few tables and plenty of TVs keep the troops entertained. (www.beerworks.net; 112 Canal St; ⊙11am-midnight; Ⓣ North Station)

Alibi

COCKTAIL BAR

18 Map p34, A4

Housed in the former Charles St Jail, this hot-to-trot drinking venue is set in the old 'drunk tank' (holding cell for the intoxicated). The prison theme is played up, with mugshots on the brick walls and iron bars on the doors and windows. Upstairs, the Lobby Bar is set under the soaring ceiling in the atrium. Both places are absurdly popular.

Local Life
Drinking in the North End
Watch football, drink Campari and speak Italian (or just listen) at **Caffè dello Sport** (Map p34, G3; www.caffe dellosport.us; 308 Hanover St; ⊙6am-midnight; Ⓣ Haymarket) or **Caffè Paradiso** (Map p34, G3; 255 Hanover St; ⊙7am-11pm; 🛜; Ⓣ Haymarket).

(www.alibiboston.com; Liberty Hotel, 215 Charles St; ⊙5pm-2am; Ⓣ Charles/MGH)

Entertainment

Improv Asylum

COMEDY

19 Map p34, F3

The basement of a CVS pharmacy is somehow a perfect setting for the dark humor spewing from the mouths of this offbeat crew. No topic is too touchy, no politics too correct. While the shows vary from night to night, the standard Mainstage Show mixes up the improv with comedy sketches that are guaranteed to make you giggle. (www.improvasylum.com; 216 Hanover St; tickets $15-25; ⊙shows 8pm Sun-Thu, 7:30pm, 10pm & midnight Fri & Sat; Ⓣ Haymarket)

TD Garden

BASKETBALL, ICE HOCKEY

20 Map p34, D2

The Garden is home to the Bruins, who play ice hockey here from September to June, and the Celtics, who play basketball from October to April. It's the city's largest venue, so big-name musicians perform here, too. (🕿 information 617-523-3030, tickets 617-931-2000; www.tdgarden.com; 150 Causeway St; Ⓣ North Station)

Shopping

In-Jean-ius

CLOTHING

21 Map p34, G2

You know what you're getting when you waltz into this denim haven.

Offerings from over 30 designers include tried-and-true favorites and little-known gems, and staff are on hand to help you find the perfect pair. Warning: the surgeon general has determined that it is not healthy to try on jeans after a gigantic plate of pasta, so shop before dinner.
(www.injeanius.com; 441 Hanover St; ⊙10am-7pm; ⊤Haymarket)

Twilight CLOTHING
22 🔒 Map p34, G3

Alison Barnard proved that she could do jeans when she opened In-jean-ius on Hanover St. She then proceeded to help her clients get frocked up, opening a slick dress shop around the corner. The purple velvet drapes and black chandeliers create an elegant atmosphere in which to browse the racks and racks of fancy wear, featuring Nicole Miller, BCBG and other high-style designers.
(www.twilightboston.com; 12 Fleet St; ⊙11am-7pm; ⊤Haymarket)

Sedurre CLOTHING
23 🔒 Map p34, G3

If you speak Italian, you'll know that Sedurre's thing is sexy and stylish (it means 'seduce'). The shop started with fine lingerie – beautiful lacy nightgowns and underthings for special occasions. Sisters Robyn and Daria were so good at that, they expanded to include dresses and evening wear (for other kinds of special occasions).
(www.sedurreboston.com; 28½ Prince St; ⊙noon-8pm Mon-Sat, to 6pm Sun; ⊤Haymarket)

North Bennet Street School HANDICRAFTS
24 🔒 Map p34, G3

The North Bennet Street School has been training craftspeople for over 100 years. Established in 1885, the school offers programs in traditional skills like book-binding, woodworking and locksmithing. The school's on-site gallery sells incredible hand-crafted pieces made by students and alumni. Look for unique jewelry, handmade journals and exquisite wooden furniture and musical instruments.
(www.nbss.org; 150 North St; ⊙9:30am-2:30pm Mon-Thu, noon-1pm Fri; ⊤North Station)

Shake the Tree JEWELRY
25 🔒 Map p34, F3

You can't know what you will find at this sweet boutique, but it's bound to be good. The little shop carries a wonderful, eclectic assortment of jewelry by local artisans, interesting stationery, designer handbags and clothing and unique housewares.
(www.shakethetreeboston.com; 67 Salem St; ⊙11am-7pm Mon-Sat, noon-5pm Sun; ⊤Haymarket)

Explore

Beacon Hill & Boston Common

Abutted by the Boston Common – the nation's original public park and the centerpiece of the city – and topped with the gold-domed Massachusetts State House, Beacon Hill is the neighborhood most often featured on Boston postcards. Aside from these two sites (which kick off the Freedom Trail), the retail and residential streets on Beacon Hill are delightfully, quintessentially Boston.

The Sights in a Day

☀️ Start your day with breakfast at the **Paramount** (p53), which should sustain you for a while. Then dedicate your morning to exploring the first few sites along the Freedom Trail, starting at the **Boston Common** (p46), touring the **Massachusetts State House** (p52) and investigating the ancient headstones in the **Granary Burying Ground** (p52).

☀️ If the weather is fine, enjoy a picnic lunch in the **Public Garden** (p52). Your afternoon is free for browsing the boutiques and shopping for antiques along **Charles St** (p55). Take a detour to marvel at the architecture on **Louisburg Square** (p53) and check out the current exhibit at the **Museum of Afro-American History** (p52).

🌙 When it's time for a break, beer-lovers should head to **Tip Tap Room** (p54) to sample from 40 kinds of craft beer, while wine drinkers might prefer **Bin 26 Enoteca** (p54). Stay for dinner or venture to one of Beacon Hill's other fine eating establishments.

 Top Sights

Boston Common (p46)

❤️ **Best of Boston**

Eating

Grotto (p53)

Drinking

Tip Tap Room (p54)

Shopping

NOA (p54)

Crush Boutique (p55)

Blackstone's of Beacon Hill (p54)

Beacon Hill Chocolates (p55)

Getting There

T Metro At the junction of the red and green lines, Park St T station services the Boston Common and sights in the southeastern part of Beacon Hill.

T Metro Also on the red line, Charles/MGH T station is convenient to Beacon Hill's Charles and Cambridge Sts, as well as the Charles River Esplanade.

Top Sights
Boston Common

The 50-acre Boston Common is the country's oldest public park. The Common has served many purposes over the years, including as a campground for British troops during the Revolutionary War and as green grass for cattle grazing until the 1830s. Although there is still a grazing ordinance on the books, the Common today serves picnickers, sunbathers and people-watchers.

👁 Map p50, E4

btwn Tremont, Charles, Beacon & Park Sts

🕑 6am–midnight

🚻

T Park St

Don't Miss

Blaxton Plaque

The Reverend William Blaxton was the first European settler of Boston. In 1634 he sold this land to the Massachusetts Bay Colony for £30. You can refer to the plaque emblazoned with the words of the treaty between Governor Winthrop and Reverend Blaxton, located at the corner of Tremont and Park Sts.

Brewer Fountain

This bronze beauty dates to 1868, when it was gifted to the city of Boston by the wealthy merchant Gardner Brewer. The fountain features four aquatic deities from antiquity: the Roman god of water, Neptune; the Greek sea goddess, Amphitrite; and the spirit Acis and the sea nymph Galatea, both from *Metamorphoses,* by the Roman poet Ovid.

Robert Gould Shaw Memorial

The magnificent bas-relief memorial (corner Beacon and Park Sts) sculpted by Augustus Saint-Gaudens honors the 54th Massachusetts Regiment of the Union Army, the nation's first all-black Civil War regiment (depicted in the 1989 film *Glory).* Shaw (the son of a wealthy Boston family) and half his men were killed in a battle at Fort Wagner, South Carolina.

Soldiers & Sailors Monument

Dedicated in 1877, this massive monument atop Flagstaff Hill pays tribute to the namesake soldiers and sailors who died in the Civil War. The four bronze statues represent Peace (facing south), the Sailor (facing the ocean), History (looking to heaven), and the Soldier (standing at ease). Many historical figures are cast in the elaborate bronze reliefs.

☑ Top Tips

▶ The Boston Common is often called 'the Common' in local parlance, but never 'the Commons.' Use the singular or risk ridicule by locals!

▶ The on-site **information tion kiosk** (GBCVB Visitors Center; www.bostonusa.com; ⏰8:30am-5pm) is a great source of information, maps, etc.

▶ The kiosk is also the starting place for guided tours by the Freedom Trail Foundation (p154).

✕ Take a Break

Various food trucks park near the entrance to the Park St T station. Our favorite is **Clover Food Lab** (www.cloverfoodlab.com). Alternatively, check out the new **Earl of Sandwich** (www.earlofsandwichusa.com; 1B Charles St, Boston Common; $7-10; ⏰9am-7pm), located in the handsome 'Pink Palace' (formerly a men's toilet, but never mind).

Understand
The Boston Massacre

In front of the Old State House (p64), encircled by cobblestones, the Boston Massacre Site marks the spot where the first blood was shed for the American independence movement. The memorial on the Boston Common commemorates the event in a more elaborate way.

On March 5, 1770, an angry mob of colonists swarmed the British soldiers guarding the State House. Sam Adams, John Hancock and about 40 other protesters hurled snowballs, rocks and insults. Thus provoked, the soldiers fired into the crowd and killed five towns people, including Crispus Attucks, a former slave.

The incident sparked enormous anti-British sentiment. Paul Revere helped fan the flames by widely disseminating an engraving that depicted the scene as an unmitigated slaughter. Interestingly, John Adams and Josiah Quincy – both of whom opposed the heavy-handed authoritarian British rule – defended the accused soldiers in court, and seven of the nine were acquitted.

Boston Massacre Monument
This 25ft monument pays tribute to the five victims of the Boston Massacre, replicating Paul Revere's famous engraving of this tragic event. Revere's effective propaganda depicts the soldiers shooting down defenseless colonists in cold blood, when in reality they were reacting to the aggressive crowd in self-defense.

Great Elm Site
A plaque marks the site of the Old Elm that stood here for more than 200 years. History has it that accused witches were hanged here and the Sons of Liberty hung lanterns on its branches as a symbol of unity. Boston's 'oldest inhabitant' was destroyed by a storm in 1876.

Frog Pond
When temperatures drop, the Boston Common becomes an urban winter wonderland, with slipping and sliding, swirling and twirling on the frozen **Frog Pond** (www.bostonfrogpond. com; adult/child admission $5/free, skate rental $9/5; ⏱10am-4pm Mon, to 9pm Tue-Thu & Sun, to 10pm Fri & Sat mid-Nov–mid-Mar; 🐾). In summer, it's a spray pool for tiny tots to cool off.

Central Burying Ground
Dating to 1756, the **Central Burying Ground** (Boylston St; ⏱9am-5pm; 🇹Boylston) is the least celebrated of the old cemeteries, as it was the burial ground of the down-and-out – according to an account in Edwin Bacon's *Boston Illustrated,* it was used for 'Roman Catholics and strangers dying in the town.' The most recognized name here is that of the notable portrait artist Gilbert Stuart.

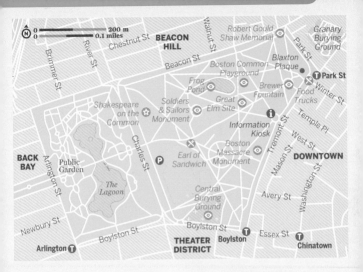

Boston Common Playground

We're not sure if America's first public park is also home to its first playground, but rest assured, this one has a huge playscape with swings, jungle gyms and a carousel.

Shakespeare on the Common

Each summer, the Commonwealth Shakespeare Company stages a major production on the Boston Common, drawing crowds for theater under the stars. **Shakespeare on the Common** (www.commshakes.org; admission free; ☺8pm Tue-Sat, 7pm Sun Jul & Aug) often appeals to the masses with a populist twist, such as *The Taming of the Shrew* set in a North End restaurant.

A B C D

1

Charles/MGH 🇹

Phillips St

Grove St

Anderson St

🔒 14

Revere St

2

Charles River

Charles River Bike Path

Pinckney St 🔒

🔒 13

Louisburg
Square

11 🔒

W Cedar St

Cedar La Way

Charles St

Acorn St

Willow St

Hatch
Memorial
Shelf

12 🔒

🗙 5

Lime St

River St

Chestnut St

Branch St

3

The
Esplanade

Embankment Rd

Brimmer St

Byron St

🚲 10

Storrow Dr

Back St

1 ◎
Public
Garden

4

Beacon St

BACK
BAY

Berkeley St

Arlington St

Charles St

Ⓟ

Marlborough St

Commonwealth Ave Mall

Ritz
Carlton
Hotel

The
Lagoon

Clarendon St

5

Commonwealth Ave

Newbury St

Boylston St

N
0 ──── 400 m
0 ──── 0.2 miles

Arlington 🇹

E

F

G

H

Cambridge St

WEST END

Garden St

Irving St

S Russell St

Joy St

Smith Ct

4
Museum of African American History

Hancock St

Ridgeway La

Temple St **9**

Bowdoin St

7

Suffolk University

Bowdoin 🚇

Cambridge St

Center Plaza

Court House

City Hall Plaza

Boston City Hall

1

Myrtle St

BEACON HILL

Derne St

Ashburton Pl

Ashburton Park

2

Somerset St

Government Center 🚇

Court St

Court Sq

State 🚇

Washington St

2

Mt Vernon St

Joy St

Massachusetts State House

Walnut St

8

School St

Tremont St

Province St

Milk St

Arch St

Beacon St

6

Park St

Granary Burying Ground

3

Bosworth St

Bromfield St

DOWNTOWN

Hawley St

Franklin St

3

Boston Common

Park St 🚇

Winter St

Cathedral Church of St Paul

Temple Pl

Snow Pl

4

Tremont St

West St

Nason St

Opera House

Washington St

Macy's

Chauncy St

Otis St

Central Burying Ground

Avery St

Millennium Place

Ave de Lafayette

Harrison Ave Ext

Boylston St

Boylston 🚇

Essex St

Chinatown 🚇

5

For reviews see	
🔴 Top Sights	p46
⊙ Sights	p52
❌ Eating	p53
🔵 Drinking	p54
🔒 Shopping	p54

Sights

Public Garden GARDENS

1 Map p50, C4

Adjoining Boston Common, the 24-acre garden provides an inviting oasis of bountiful flowers and shady trees. Its centerpiece, a tranquil lagoon with old-fashioned, pedal-powered **Swan Boats** (www.swanboats.com; Public Garden; adult/child/senior $2.75/1.50/2; ☺10am-4pm, to 5pm mid-Jun–Aug; ⓣArlington), has been delighting children for generations. (www.friendsofthepublicgarden.org; btwn Charles, Beacon, Boylston & Arlington Sts; ☺6am-midnight; ♿; ⓣArlington)

Massachusetts State House NOTABLE BUILDING

2 Map p50, F2

Charles Bulfinch designed the commanding state capitol, but Oliver

✓ **Top Tip**

Black Heritage Trail

The 1.6-mile **Black Heritage Trail** (www.nps.gov/boaf; admission free; ☺tours 2pm Mon-Sat Mar-Nov, more frequently in summer; ⓣPark St) tour explores the history of the abolitionist movement and African American settlement on Beacon Hill. The NPS conducts guided tours, but maps and descriptions for self-guided tours are available at the Museum of African American History (or on the website).

Wendell Holmes called it 'the hub of the solar system' (thus earning Boston the nickname 'the Hub'). Call to reserve a free 40-minute tour covering the history, artwork, architecture and political personalities of the State House, as well as a visit to the legislative chambers. (☎617-727-3676; www.sec.state.ma.us; cnr Beacon & Bowdoin Sts; admission free; ☺9am-5pm, tours 10am-3:30pm Mon-Fri; ⓣPark St)

Granary Burying Ground CEMETERY

3 Map p50, G3

Dating to 1660, this atmospheric atoll is crammed with historic headstones, many with evocative (and creepy) carvings. This is the final resting place of all your favorite revolutionary heroes, including Paul Revere, Sam Adams, John Hancock and James Otis. Benjamin Franklin is buried in Philadelphia, but the Franklin family plot here contains his parents. (Tremont St; ☺9am-5pm; ⓣPark St)

Museum of African American History MUSEUM

4 Map p50, E1

Beacon Hill was never the exclusive domain of blue-blooded Bostonians; in the 19th century, freed African Americans settled on the back side of the hill. Rotating exhibits are set in two adjacent historic buildings: the African Meeting House, the country's oldest black church and meeting house; and Abiel Smith School, the country's first school for blacks.

(www.afroammuseum.org; 46 Joy St; adult/
senior/child $5/3/free; ⊙10am-4pm Mon-
Sat; **T** Park St or Bowdoin)

Eating

Paramount
CAFETERIA $

5 Map p50, C3

This old-fashioned cafeteria is a
neighborhood favorite, especially
for brunch. Basic diner fare includes
pancakes, steak and eggs, burgers and
sandwiches, and big, hearty salads.
For dinner they add table service and
candlelight – the place goes upscale
without losing its down-home charm.
(www.paramountboston.com; 44 Charles
St; breakfast & lunch $8-12, dinner $15-30;
⊙7am-10pm Mon-Thu, from 8am Sat & Sun,
to 11pm Fri & Sat; 🍴🚸; **T** Charles/MGH)

No 9 Park
EUROPEAN $$$

6 Map p50, F3

Set in a 19th-century mansion op-
posite the State House, this swanky
place tops fine-dining lists. Chef-
owner Barbara Lynch has been lauded
by food and wine magazines for her
delectable French and Italian culinary
masterpieces and first-rate wine list.
She has since cast her celebrity-chef
spell all around town, but this is the
place that made her famous. Reserva-
tions recommended.
(📞617-742-9991; www.no9park.com; 9 Park
St; mains $39, 3-course prix fixe $69; ⊙Sun
& Mon 5:30-9pm, Tue-Sat to 10pm; **T** Park St)

Hidden Beacon Hill

Take a detour away from Charles St
to discover a few Beacon Hill gems.
There is no more prestigious ad-
dress than **Louisburg Sq** (**T** Charles/
MGH), a cluster of stately brick row
houses facing a private park. Nearby
Acorn St (**T** Charles/MGH) is Bos-
ton's oft-photographed narrowest
street. This cobblestone alleyway
was once home to artisans and to
the service people who worked for
the adjacent mansion dwellers.

Grotto
ITALIAN $$

7 Map p50, F1

Tucked into a basement on the back
side of Beacon Hill, this cozy, cave-
like place lives up to its name. The funky
decor – exposed brick walls decked
with rotating art exhibits – reflects the
innovative menu, which also changes
frequently. Reserve for dinner.
(📞617-227-3434; www.grottorestaurant.com;
37 Bowdoin St; mains $21, 3-course prix fixe
$35; ⊙11:30am-3pm Mon-Fri, 5-10pm daily;
T Bowdoin)

Scollay Square
AMERICAN $$

8 Map p50, G2

Down the road from the former Scollay
Sq, this retro restaurant hearkens back
to the glory days of its namesake. Old
photos and memorabilia adorn the
walls, while suits sip martinis to big-
band music. The classic American fare

is reliably good, with the lobster mac-and-cheese as the perennial favorite. (www.scollaysquare.com; 21 Beacon St; lunch mains $10-16, dinner mains $17-23; ⏲lunch Mon-Fri, brunch Sat & Sun, dinner daily; ⓣPark St)

Drinking

Tip Tap Room   BAR

9 Map p50, F1

The 'tips' are steak, lamb, turkey, chicken or swordfish. The 'taps' are nearly 40 kinds of beer, ranging from local craft brews to international ales. With a long, L-shaped bar and big windows overlooking Cambridge St, the Tip Tap Room has quickly become a neighborhood favorite for its trendy but friendly vibe; it's especially popular with the after-work crowd. (www.thetiptaproom.com; 138 Cambridge St; ⏲11:30am-2am Mon-Sat, 10:30am-2am Sun; �📶; ⓣCharles/MGH or Bowdoin)

Local Life

21st Amendment

Named for one of the US Constitution's most important amendments (the one that repealed Prohibition), **21st Amendment** (Map p51, F2; www.21stboston.com; 150 Bowdoin St; ⏲11:30am-10pm Sun-Thu, to 11pm Fri & Sat; ⓣPark St) has been an ever-popular haunt for overeducated and underpaid statehouse workers to meet up and whinge about the wheels of government.

Bin 26 Enoteca   WINE BAR

10 🚇 Map p50, C3

If you are into your wine, you'll be into the Bin. Big windows overlook Charles St and wine bottles line the walls. The 60-page wine list spans the globe, including a moderately priced house wine bottled in Italy just for the restaurant. Staff will insist you order food (due to licensing requirements) but you won't regret sampling the simple, seasonal menu. (☎617-723-5939; www.bin26.com; 26 Charles St; ⏲noon-10pm; ⓣCharles/MGH)

Shopping

NOA   JEWELRY, HANDICRAFTS

11 🔒 Map p50, C2

Candles, glassware, jewelry, furniture, handbags, mobiles, mosaics, photography, pottery, soaps, stationary, woodwork and more. And all of it – *all* of it – made by local artists. (www.noagifts.com; 88 Charles St; ⏲11am-7pm Mon-Fri, 10am-6pm Sat, noon-6pm Sun; ⓣCharles/MGH)

Blackstone's of Beacon Hill   GIFTS, ACCESSORIES

12 🔒 Map p50, C3

Here's a guarantee: you will find the perfect gift for that certain someone at Blackstone's. This little place is crammed with classy, clever and otherwise unusual items. Bestsellers include books by local authors and locally made handicrafts, as well as

Antiquing on Beacon Hill

There was a time when Charles St was lined with antique shops and nothing else: some historians claim that the country's antique trade began right here on Beacon Hill. Many vestiges remain from these days of yesteryear. Here are a few of our favorites:

Eugene Galleries (Map p50, C2; www.eugenegalleries.com; 76 Charles St; ⊙11am-6pm Mon-Sat, noon-6pm Sun; ⊤Charles/MGH) A tiny shop with a remarkable selection of old prints and maps, especially focusing on old Boston.

Marika's Antique Shop (Map p50, C1; 130 Charles St; ⊤Charles/MGH) A treasure trove of jewelry, silver and porcelain.

Twentieth Century Ltd (Map p50, C2; www.boston-vintagejewelry.com; 73 Charles St; ⊤Charles/MGH) Vintage costume jewelry, made by the great designers of yesteryear.

quirky, Boston-themed souvenirs like clocks and coasters. Otherwise, you can't go wrong with a solar-powered rotating globe – everyone needs one! (www.blackstonesbeaconhill.com; 46 Charles St; ⊙10am-6:30pm Mon-Sat, 11am-5pm Sun; ⊤Charles/MGH)

Beacon Hill Chocolates
FOOD & DRINK

13 🔒 Map p50, C2

This artisanal chocolatier puts equal effort into selecting fine chocolates from around the world and designing beautiful keepsake boxes to contain them. Using decoupage to affix old postcards, photos and illustrations, the boxes are works of art even before they are filled with truffles. Pick out an image of Historic Boston as a souvenir for the sweet tooth in your life.

(www.beaconhillchocolates.com; 91 Charles St; ⊙11am-7pm Mon-Sat, noon-5:30pm Sun; ⊤Charles/MGH)

Crush Boutique
CLOTHING

14 🔒 Map p50, C1

Fashion mavens rave about this cute, cozy basement boutique on Charles St, which features both well-loved designers and up-and-coming talents. The selection of clothing is excellent, but it's the expert advice that makes this place so popular. Co-owners (and childhood BFFs) Rebecca and Laura would love to help you find something that makes you look fabulous. (www.shopcrushboutique.com; 131 Charles St; ⊤Charles/MGH)

Explore

Downtown & Waterfront

Much of Boston's business and tourist activity takes place in this central downtown neighborhood, which is crammed with historic sites and waterside attractions. Across the Fort Point Channel, the Seaport District is fast developing as a waterside destination, thanks to the dynamic contemporary art museum and an explosion of new dining options.

The Sights in a Day

☀ The Freedom Trail cuts right through downtown Boston. You can spend your morning seeing some of the city's most important historic sites, including the **Old South Meeting House** (p64), **Old State House** (p64) and **Faneuil Hall** (p65). By lunch time, you're right in the vicinity of **Quincy Market** (p68).

☀ After lunch, stroll along the **Rose Kennedy Greenway** (p64) to reach the Waterfront. If you're up for more history, head to the **Boston Tea Party Ships & Museum** (p64). If you're ready for a change of pace, opt to visit the sea creatures at the **New England Aquarium** (p58) or to peruse the diverse creations at the **Institute of Contemporary Art** (p60).

☾ You're in the right place for dinner, as the Seaport District is home to some of Boston's hottest restaurants. Go to **Sam's** (p67) for the view or **Row 34** (p67) for the scene. Finish the night with something delicious created by the mixologists at **Drink** (p68).

👁 Top Sights

New England Aquarium (p58)

Institute of Contemporary Art (p60)

♥ Best of Boston

Eating

Row 34 (p67)

Sam's at Louis (p67)

Yankee Lobster Co (p67)

City Landing (p68)

Drinking

Drink (p68)

Thinking Cup (p68)

Harpoon Brewery (p70)

Last Hurrah (p70)

Getting There

🇹 **Metro** All of the metro lines traverse this central neighborhood, with useful stops at Haymarket (for Faneuil Hall), State (the Aquarium) and South Station (the Seaport District).

🚌 **Bus** The silver-line bus SL1 runs from South Station into the Seaport District.

⚓ **Boat** City Water Taxi stops at Long Wharf on the waterfront.

Top Sights
New England Aquarium

Teeming with sea creatures of all sizes, shapes and colors, this giant fishbowl is the centerpiece of downtown Boston's waterfront. The main attraction is the newly renovated, three-story Giant Ocean Tank, which swirls with thousands of creatures great and small, including turtles, sharks and eels. Countless side exhibits explore the lives and habitats of other underwater oddities, as well as penguins and sea mammals.

⊙ Map p62, E2

www.neaq.org

Central Wharf

adult/child $23/16

⊘9am-5pm Mon-Fri, to 6pm Sat & Sun, 1hr later Jul & Aug

Ⓣ Aquarium

Seals at the New England Aquarium

Don't Miss

Shark & Ray Touch Tank

The awesome Shark & Ray Touch Tank recreates a mangrove swamp teeming with Atlantic rays, cownose rays, bonnethead sharks and epaulette sharks. The huge tank is at waist-level, which allows visitors to dip a hand in and feel the smooth skin of the sea creatures sliding past.

Jellyfish

Descend to the lower level to discover a room full of ethereal sea jellies. Despite having no bones, brains or hearts, these captivating species have somehow managed to survive for millions of years.

Penguins

Most of the aquarium's 1st floor is occupied by an enormous penguin exhibit, home to three different species and more than 80 birds. Throughout the day, visitors can see live demonstrations and feedings.

Marine Mammals

Harbor seals frolic in a large observation tank near the aquarium entrance, while the inside facility is home to northern fur seals. Both groups of pinnipeds put on an entertaining show without much prodding. The open-air Marine Mammal Center is set up for daily training demonstrations.

Amazon Rainforest

Six different tanks showcase the flora and fauna of the Amazon rainforest, including piranhas, anacondas, electric eels and poison dart frogs. The exhibits also emphasize the importance of sustainable fishing practices.

☑ **Top Tips**

▶ Buy timed tickets in advance to skip the lines (the 9am slot is best for avoiding crowds).

▶ The 3D **Simons IMAX Theatre** (www.neaq.org; Central Wharf; adult/senior & child $10/8; ⊙ 10am-10pm; ⊕; T Aquarium) features films with aquatic themes.

▶ The aquarium organizes whale-watching cruises (p66). Combination tickets are available.

✕ **Take a Break**

There are several options for lunch on Aquarium Plaza, including the **Reef** (www.neaq.org; Aquarium Plaza; mains $9-16; ⊙ 11:30am-9pm May-Oct; ✔ ⊕; T Aquarium), a seasonal outdoor restaurant serving lobster rolls, clam chowder and steamers, with a side of sea breezes.

Nearby, classy **City Landing** (p68) is a full-service restaurant that offers something to suit every palate.

Top Sights
Institute of Contemporary Art

Boston is becoming a focal point for contemporary art in the 21st century, as hundreds of thousands of visitors flock to the dramatic quarters of the Institute of Contemporary Art. The building is a work of art in itself – a striking glass structure cantilevered over a waterside plaza. The spacious light-filled interior hosts multimedia presentations, educational programs and studio space. More importantly, it is the venue for the development of the ICA's permanent collection of 21st-century art.

◉ Map p62, F3

www.icaboston.org

100 Northern Ave

adult/child/student/senior $15/free/10/13

⊙10am-5pm Tue, Wed, Sat & Sun, to 9pm Thu & Fri

🚌SL1 or SL2, 🇹South Station

Don't Miss

Founders Gallery

Arguably, the ICA building and setting are as much of an attraction as the art. Opened in 2006, the structure skillfully incorporates its surroundings into the architecture. In the Founders Gallery, which spans the entire width of the building, a glass wall virtually eliminates any barrier between viewer and seascape.

Permanent Collection

In addition to dynamic temporary exhibits, the ICA showcases national and international artists in its permanent collection. You'll find the likes of graffiti-artist Shepard Fairey, video artist Christian Jankowski, photographer Boris Mikhailov, local boy Josiah McElhany and sculptor Tara Donovan. Look for all manner of art, from painting to video to multidimensional mixed-media mash-ups.

Mediatheque

The Mediatheque is the museum's digital media center, where visitors can use the computer stations to learn more about featured art and artists. The terraced room also has a wall of windows at the front, but the room's unique perspective shows only the dancing and rippling of water, with no horizon in sight.

Barbara Lee Family Foundation Theater

The Barbara Lee Family Foundation Theater is one of the ICA's coolest features. With wooden floor and ceiling and glass walls, the two-story venue is an extension of the boardwalk outside. It's a remarkable backdrop for edgy theater, dance, music and other performance art.

☑ Top Tips

▶ Take advantage of the ICA audio commentary that is available free with admission. Borrow an iPod from the front desk or download the tracks to your own MP3 player from the museum website.

▶ The ICA offers guided thematic tours on Saturday and Sunday (1pm and 2:30pm) and Thursday evenings (6pm and 7pm).

▶ Admission is free for all on Thursdays after 5pm.

▶ Admission is always free for youth age 17 and under.

✕ Take a Break

At the ICA, the **Water Cafe** (⊙ 11am-4pm Tue-Sun, to 8pm Thu-Fri) is a simple affair, featuring harbor views and food by Wolfgang Puck. If you prefer to leave the museum, it's a short stroll to **Sam's at Louis** (p67).

A

B

C

D

1

T Bowdoin

Cambridge St

New Sudbury St

Haymarket
T

2
John F Fitzgerald Surface Rd

Rose Kennedy Greenway

Atlantic Ave

Joy St

Hancock St

Bowdoin St

Somerset St

City Hall Plaza

Boston City Hall

Faneuil Hall

14

WATERFRON

Myrtle St

Government Center
T

15 24

Quincy Market

Aquariu
T 13

Massachusetts State House

State St

State
T 3

Old State House

23

Purchase St

Atlantic Ave

Mt Vernon St

King's Chapel & Burying Ground 5

DOWNTOWN

Kilby St

Water St

India St

Broad St

Batterymarch St

Beacon St

School St

19

Liberty Square

High St

2

Park St

Tremont St

Old South Meeting House 4

Milk St

Devonshire St

Franklin St

Pearl St

Oliver St

Wharf District Parks

Park St
T

Winter St

Downtown Crossing
T

Hawley St

Federal St

Boston Common

Temple Pl

West St

Washington St

Macy's

Arch St

Otis St

Summer St

Matthews St

High St

Dewey Sq Parks

Congress St

3

17

21 22

Avery St

Chauncy St

20

Bedford St

Kingston St

Atlantic Ave

Boston Te Party Ship & Museur

Millennium Place

Ave de Lafayette

Boylston St
T
Boylston

Essex St

Chinatown
T

One Financial Place

South Station
T

South Station

1

Congress St Bridge

THEATER DISTRICT

Beach St

Tufts St

Stuart St

Harrison Ave

Tyler St

Hudson St

Surface Rd

LEATHER DISTRICT

US South Boston Postal Annex

Summer St Bridge

New England Medical Center
T

Kneeland St

4

Washington St

Harvard St

Lincoln St

Dorchester Ave

Fort Point Channel

Acco C

Tremont St

CHINATOWN

Oak St W

Marginal Rd

5

Massachusetts Turnpike

For reviews see

◉ Top Sights	p58
◉ Sights	p64
✖ Eating	p67
☕ Drinking	p68
✪ Entertainment	p70
🔒 Shopping	p71

0
N
0
500 m
0.25 miles

City Water Taxi

Ferry to Boston Harbor
Islands State Park

New England Aquarium

w England
quarium
ale Watch

Boston Inner Harbor

Airport Water Shuttle

Rowes Wharf
Water Taxi

d Northern
ve Bridge — Harbour Walk

elyn
akley
dge 🔟 12

Moakley Federal
Courthouse

Fan
Pier 🔟 10

Northern Ave

Marine Park Dr

*Institute of
Contemporary
Art*
◉

Bay State Cruise Co

World
Trade
Center

Sleeper St

**SEAPORT
DISTRICT**
P

Thomson Pl

Fish
Pier

Boston
Children's
Museum
🔟 16

Stillings St

Boston Wharf Rd

P

E Service Rd

Commonwealth
Pier

Seaport Blvd

B St

AC Cruise Line

Summer St

9 ✖

Congress St

W Service Rd

11 ✖

*Boston Convention
& Exhibition Center*

18 ☕

Sights

Boston Tea Party Ships & Museum
MUSEUM

1 Map p62, D4

Handsome replicas of the Tea Party Ships are moored at the reconstructed Griffin's Wharf, alongside a shiny museum dedicated to the revolution's most catalytic event. Interactive exhibits allows visitors to meet re-enactors in period costume, explore the ships, learn about contemporary popular perceptions through multimedia presentations, and even participate in the protest. (www.bostonteapartyship.com; Congress St Bridge; adult/child $25/15; ⏱ 10am-5pm, last tour 4pm; ♿; T South Station)

Rose Kennedy Greenway
PARK

2 Map p62, C1

Upon completion of the infamous Central Artery Project, aka the Big Dig, the city reclaimed 27 acres for pleasant parks and civic plazas, now hosting art markets, food trucks and more. The Ring Fountain is a cool place for visitors to rest and recover. There's also a walking labyrinth for the contemplative and a Boston-themed carousel for the kiddies. (www.rosekennedygreenway.org; ♿; T Aquarium or Haymarket)

Old State House
HISTORIC BUILDING

3 Map p62, C2

Dating to 1713, the Old State House is Boston's oldest surviving public building. The building is best known for its balcony, where the Declaration of Independence was first read to Bostonians in 1776. Inside, the Old State House contains a small museum of revolutionary memorabilia, with videos and multimedia presentations about the Boston Massacre, which took place out front. (www.bostonhistory.org; 206 Washington St; adult/child/senior & student $10/free/$8.50; ⏱9am-5pm; ♿; T State)

Old South Meeting House
HISTORIC BUILDING

4 Map p62, C2

'No tax on tea!' That was the decision on December 16, 1773, when 5000 angry colonists gathered here to protest against British taxes, leading to the Boston Tea Party. Visit the graceful meeting house to see an exhibit about the history of the building and listen to an audio re-creation of the historic pre–Tea Party meeting. (www.osmh.org; 310 Washington St; adult/child/senior & student $6/1/5; ⏱9:30am-

---

✅ Top Tip

Freedom Trail Ticket

If you are following the red brick road, consider purchasing the Freedom Trail Ticket (adult/child $13/2), which includes admission to the Old State House, the Old South Meeting House and the Paul Revere House.

Old State House

5pm Apr-Oct, 10am-4pm Nov-Mar; ;
Ⓣ Downtown Crossing or State)

King's Chapel & Burying Ground   CHURCH, CEMETERY

5 ◎ Map p62, B2

Bostonians were not pleased when the original Anglican church was erected on this site in 1688. The granite chapel standing today – built in 1754 – houses the largest bell ever made by Paul Revere, as well as a historic organ. The adjacent burying ground is the oldest in the city, with headstones dating to 1623.
(www.kings-chapel.org; 58 Tremont St; self-guided tour $2 donation, Bells & Bones tours

$5-8; ◷10am-4pm Mon-Sat & 1:30-4pm Sun;
Ⓣ Park St)

Faneuil Hall   HISTORIC BUILDING

6 ◎ Map p62, C1

'Those who cannot bear free speech had best go home,' said Wendell Phillips. 'Faneuil Hall is no place for slavish hearts.' Indeed, this public meeting place was the site of so much revolutionary rabble-rousing that it earned the nickname the 'Cradle of Liberty.' It's normally open to the public, who can hear about the building's history from NPS rangers.
(www.faneuilhall.com; Congress St; admission free; ◷9am-5pm; Ⓣ Haymarket or Aquarium)

Understand
Boston Tea Party

In May 1773, the British Parliament passed the Tea Act, granting a trade monopoly to the East India Company, thus requiring colonists to pay additional taxes on their tea. In December, three tea-bearing vessels arrived in Boston Harbor, but colonial merchants refused the shipments. When they tried to depart, the loyalist Governor Hutchinson demanded their cargo be unloaded.

At a meeting in the Old South Church, the Sons of Liberty decided to take matters into their own hands. Disguised as Mohawk Indians, they descended on the waterfront, boarded the ships and dumped 90,000 pounds of taxable tea into the harbor.

The king's retribution was swift. Legislation was rushed through Parliament to punish Boston, 'the center of rebellious commotion in America, the ring leader in every riot.' The port was blockaded and the city was placed under military rule, which further fueled tensions between colonists and the king.

Boston Children's Museum

MUSEUM

7 Map p62, E4

If you're traveling with small children, don't miss the interactive, educational exhibits at this museum. Young audience members are invited to participate in the performances at the children's theater, and the light-filled atrium features an amazing 3-story climbing structure where you might lose them for hours. Other highlights include a bubble exhibit, a hands-on construction site and intercultural immersion experiences. (www.bostonchildrensmuseum.org; 300 Congress St; admission $14, Fri evening $1; ☺10am-5pm Sat-Thu, to 9pm Fri; 🚼; T South Station)

New England Aquarium Whale Watch

WHALE WATCHING

8 Map p62, E2

Board the *Voyager III* for the journey out to Stellwagen Bank, a rich feeding ground for whales, dolphins and marine birds. Onboard naturalists can answer all your questions, plus they have keen eyes. Whale sightings are guaranteed; otherwise, you receive a coupon for a free trip at a later date. (www.neaq.org; Central Wharf; adult/child/infant $47/32/16; ☺10am Apr-Oct, additional cruises May-Sep; 🚼; T Aquarium)

Eating

Row 34
SEAFOOD $$$

9 Map p62, E4

In the heart of the new Seaport District, this is a 'working man's oyster bar' (by working man, they mean yuppie). Set in a sharp, post-industrial space, the place offers a dozen types of raw oysters and clams, alongside an amazing selection of craft beers. (☑617-553-5900; www.row34.com; 383 Congress St; oysters $2-3, lunch mains $13-18, dinner mains $21-28; ⊙11:30am-10pm Mon-Fri, 5-10pm Sat & Sun; Ⓣ South Station)

Sam's at Louis
MODERN AMERICAN $$$

10 Map p62, F3

Unarguably, the highlight of Sam's is the three walls of windows, yielding a 180-degree view of city and sea. Chrome and leather, post-industrial decor complements this spectacular view. It's a delightfully casual-chic place, with an interesting, innovative menu to match. (☑617-295-0191; www.samsatlouis.com; 60 Northern Ave; sandwiches $13-16, mains $25-30; ⊙11:30am-10pm Mon-Thu, to 11pm Fri & Sat, 11am-9pm Sun; Ⓟ 🛜 🗒; ▢ SL1 or SL2, Ⓣ South Station)

Yankee Lobster Co
SEAFOOD $$

11 Map p62, H5

The Zanti family has been fishing for three generations, so they definitely know their stuff. This retail fish market is scattered with a few tables in case you want to dine in. And you do. Order something simple such as a lobster roll, accompany it with a cold beer and you will not be disappointed. (www.yankeelobstercompany.com; 300 Northern Ave; mains $11-20; ⊙10am-9pm Mon-Sat, 11am-6pm Sun; ▢ SL1 or SL2, Ⓣ South Station)

Barking Crab
SEAFOOD $$

12 Map p62, E3

Big buckets of crabs (Jonah, blue, snow, Alaskan etc), steamers dripping in lemon and butter, paper plates piled high with all things fried... The food here is plentiful and cheap, and you eat it at communal picnic tables overlooking the water. Beer flows

---

Local Life
Downtown Lunch Break

Where do locals go on their lunch break? **Casa Razdora** (Map p62, C2; www.casarazdora.com; 115 Water St; mains $6-10; ⊙ lunch Mon-Fri; 🗒; Ⓣ State) is a local favorite for housemade pasta topped with fresh sauces. **Falafel King** (Map p62, B2; 48 Winter St; mains $5-7; ⊙ 11am-8pm Mon-Fri, to 4pm Sat; 🗒; Ⓣ Downtown Crossing) serves 'em up quick and dirty. For good old-fashioned sandwiches, head to **Sam La Grassa's** (Map 62, B2; www.samlagrassas.com; 44 Province St; sandwiches $11; ⊙ lunch Mon-Fri; 🛒; Ⓣ Downtown Crossing) and be prepared to share a table.

freely. Service is slack, but the atmosphere is jovial.
(www.barkingcrab.com; 88 Sleeper St; sandwiches $9-18, mains $14-24; ⏱11:30am-10pm Sun-Wed, to 11pm Thu-Sat; 🚊SL1 or SL2, Ⓣ South Station or Aquarium)

City Landing

AMERICAN $$$

15 Map p62, D2

Chef Bill Brodsky promises something for everyone at this stylish venue, which features special gluten-free, veggie and children's menus. Highlighting local ingredients, you'll find innovative salads, satisfying pizzettas and sophisticated entrees.
(☎ 617-725-0305; www.citylanding.com; 255 State St; lunch mains $14-20, dinner mains $20-30; ⏱11:30am-10pm Mon-Sat, 9:30am-9pm Sun; 🖋 ♿; Ⓣ Aquarium)

Union Oyster House

SEAFOOD $$$

14 Map p62, C1

The oldest restaurant in America, ye olde Union Oyster House has been serving seafood in this historic building since 1826. Countless history-makers have propped themselves up at this bar, including Daniel Webster and John F Kennedy. Squeeze yourself into a tiny booth and devour a bowl of delicious clam chowder, or sit at the original oyster bar and watch the shucker work his magic.
(www.unionoysterhouse.com; 41 Union St; lunch mains $15-20, dinner mains $22-32; ⏱11am-9:30pm; Ⓣ Haymarket)

Quincy Market

FOOD COURT $

15 Map p62, C1

Behind Faneuil Hall, this marketplace offers a variety of options under one roof: the place is packed with about 20 restaurants and 40 food stalls. Choose from chowder, bagels, Indian, Greek, baked goods, ice cream and more, and take a seat at one of the tables in the central rotunda.
(Congress St; ⏱10am-9pm Mon-Sat, noon-6pm Sun; 🖋 ♿; Ⓣ Haymarket)

Drinking

Drink

COCKTAIL BAR

16 Map p62, F4

There is no cocktail menu at Drink. Instead you have a little chat with the bartender, and he or she will whip something up according to your specifications. The bar takes seriously the art of drink mixology – and you will too, after you sample one of its concoctions. The subterranean space creates a dark, sexy atmosphere, which makes for a great date destination.
(www.drinkfortpoint.com; 348 Congress St S; ⏱4pm-1am; 🚊SL1 or SL2, Ⓣ South Station)

Thinking Cup

CAFE

17 Map p62, A3

There are a few things that make the Thinking Cup special. One is the French hot chocolate – ooh la la. Another is the Stumptown Coffee, the

Understand

Seafood

- -

A word to the wise: when in Boston, eat as much seafood as possible. Here's a quick guide to the New England classics.

Chowder

Ask ten locals for Boston's best chowder and you'll get ten different answers. This thick, cream-based soup is chock-full of clams or fish, although clam chowder, using the meaty insides of giant surf clams, is more prevalent. Sample it at Union Oyster House (p68).

Clams & Oysters

Many seafood restaurants showcase their shellfish at a raw bar, where a dedicated bartender works to shuck raw oysters and clams to be served on the half-shell. Any self-respecting raw bar will have a selection of hard-shelled clams, or 'quahogs,' including littlenecks and cherrystones. The most famous type of oysters are Wellfleet oysters from Cape Cod; they're eaten raw, with a dollop of cocktail sauce and a few drops of lemon juice. For your own raw bar experience, head to Row 34 (p67). You can also get clams deep-fried (great hangover food) or steamed (aka 'steamers').

Lobster

Back in the day, the seemingly endless supply of lobster was the food of poor people and prisoners. Now seafood lovers pay big bucks for the crustaceans. Traditionally, lobsters are steamed or boiled, then it's up to the hungry patron to crack the shell to get the succulent meat out. A less labor-intensive choice is a lobster roll, where the lobster meat is dressed with a little mayonnaise and stuffed into a grilled, buttered hot-dog roll. Either way, you can't go wrong at Yankee Lobster Co (p67).

Fish

Atlantic Codfish has played such an important role in the region's culture and economy that it is known as the 'sacred cod,' and a carved wooden effigy hangs in the Massachusetts State House. Cod, haddock, hake and other white-fleshed fish are sometimes called 'scrod.' Other fresh local fishes appearing on Boston menus in summer include bluefin tuna, bluefish and striped bass, eg at Atlantic Fish Co (p103).

Portland brew that has earned accolades from coffee-drinkers around the country. But the best thing? It's across from the Boston Common, making it a perfect stop for a post–Frog Pond warm-up.

(www.thinkingcup.com; 165 Tremont St; ⊙7am-10pm Mon-Wed, to 11pm Thu-Sun; Ⓣ Boylston)

Harpoon Brewery BREWERY

18 Ⓣ Map p62, H5

This brewery is the largest beer facility in the state. Complimentary tastings take place in a room overlooking the brewery, while the weekend tours provide an overview of the brewing process (also with samples). Tours last about one hour and they often sell out, so don't come too late in the day. (www.harpoonbrewery.com; 306 Northern Ave; admission free; ⊙tastings 2pm & 4pm Mon-Fri, tours 10:30am-5pm Sat & 11:30am-3pm Sun; Ⓡ SL1 or SL2, Ⓣ South Station)

Local Life
Lucky's Lounge

You know it's a local hangout when they don't bother to put up a sign outside. **Lucky's Lounge** (Map p62, C1, www.luckyslounge.com, 355 Congress St S; ⊙11am-2am Sun-Fri, 6pm-2am Sat; Ⓡ SL1 or SL2, Ⓣ South Station) is a delightfully gritty lounge that's straight from 1959. Enjoy excellent martinis and Motown-inspired bands (Wednesday to Friday). Saturday and Sunday are dedicated to Sinatra.

Last Hurrah BAR

19 Ⓣ Map pG2, D2

It's now named for the 1956 novel about former Boston mayor James Michael Curley, but the beautiful lobby bar of the Omni Parker House hotel was a hallowed haunt for Boston's 19th-century intelligentsia and politicians. Enjoy a dish of hot nuts and drink a bourbon at this throwback to Old Boston.

(www.omnihotels.com; 60 School St; ⊙11:30am-12:30am Mon-Fri, 4:30-11:30pm Sat; Ⓣ Park St)

Good Life CLUB

20 Ⓣ Map p62, B3

The Good Life means a lot of things to a lot of people – solid lunch option, after-work hangout, etc. But the top reason to come to the Good Life is to get your groove on. Two bars on two floors, and great DJs spinning tunes. Wednesday is open-mic night, and the dancing goes down Thursday through Saturday.

(www.goodlifebar.com; 28 Kingston St; cover $5; ⊙11:30am-2am Mon-Fri, 6pm-2am Sat; Ⓣ Downtown Crossing)

Entertainment

Opera House LIVE PERFORMANCE

21 ☆ Map p62, B3

This lavish theater has been restored to its 1928 glory, complete with mural-painted ceiling, gilded molding and plush velvet curtains. The glitzy venue regularly hosts productions from the Broadway Across America series, and is also the main performance space for the Boston Ballet. (www.bostonoperahouse.com; 539 Washington St; TDowntown Crossing)

Paramount Center DANCE, THEATER

22 Map p62, B3

This art-deco masterpiece, restored by Emerson College, re-opened in 2010. Originally a 1700-seat, single-screen cinema, it was owned by Paramount Pictures (thus, the name). The new facility includes a cinema and a black-box stage, as well as the more traditional but still grand theater space. (www.artsemerson.org; 559 Washington St; TDowntown Crossing)

Shopping

Greenway Open Market ART MARKET

23 🔒 Map p62, D2

One of the newest features on the Greenway, the Saturday-only Open Market brings dozens of vendors to display their wares in the open air. Look for unique, handmade gifts, jewelry, bags, paintings, ceramics and other arts and crafts – most of which are locally and ethically made. (www.greenwayopenmarket.com; Surface Ave; ⏱11am-5pm Sat May-Oct; 🛜; TAquarium)

🔵 Local Life
Brattle Bookshop

Since 1825, the **Brattle Book Shop** (Map p62, B3; www.brattlebookshop.com; 9 West St; ⏱9am-5:30pm Mon-Sat; TPark St) has catered to Boston's literati: it's a treasure trove crammed with out-of-print, rare and first-edition books. Ken Gloss – whose family has owned this gem since 1949 – is an expert on antiquarian books (you'll see him on *Antiques Roadshow*). Don't miss the bargains in the outside lot.

Quincy Market ART MARKET

24 🔒 Map p62, D2

Once a meat and produce market, now a festive shopping center, the three historic market buildings are home to dozens of shops. Some are national chains, while others are Boston originals. Top spots for souvenirs include **Lucy's League** (www.thecolorstores.com; North Bldg, Faneuil Hall; TGovernment Center) for stylish sports gear, **Geoclassics** (www.geoclassics.com; 7 North Market; TState) for unique jewelry and **Funusual** (www.funusual.com; 8 North Bldg, Faneuil Hall; TGovernment Center) for toys and novelties. (www.faneuilhallmarketplace.com; ⏱10am-9pm Mon-Sat, noon-6pm Sun; 🛜; THaymarket)

Top Sights
Boston Harbor Islands

Getting There

🚢 Boston Harbor Cruises offers seasonal ferry service (adult/child $15/9) from Long Wharf to Spectacle Island or to Georges Island, from where the inter-island shuttle runs to the smaller islands.

Boston Harbor is sprinkled with 34 islands, many of which are open for trail walking, bird-watching, fishing and swimming. The Boston Harbor Islands offer a range of ecosystems – sandy beaches, rocky cliffs, fresh- and saltwater marshes and forested trails – only 45 minutes from downtown Boston. Since the massive, multimillion-dollar cleanup of Boston Harbor in the mid-1990s, the islands are one of the city's most magnificent natural assets.

Peddocks Island (p74)

Don't Miss

Boston Harbor Islands Pavilion
Ideally located on the Rose Kennedy Greenway, this information center (p160) will tell you everything you need to know to plan your visit to the Boston Harbor Islands.

Georges Island
Georges Island is the transportation hub for the islands. It is also the site of Fort Warren, a 19th-century fort and Civil War prison. While National Park Service (NPS) rangers give guided tours of the fort and there is a small museum, it is largely abandoned, with many dark tunnels, creepy corners and magnificent lookouts to discover.

Spectacle Island
A Harbor Islands hub, Spectacle Island has a large marina, a solar-powered visitor center, a healthy snack bar and supervised beaches. Five miles of walking trails provide access to a 157ft peak overlooking the harbor. Spectacle Island is also the starting point for sea-kayak outings led by park rangers in July and August.

Lovells Island
Two deadly shipwrecks may bode badly for seafarers, but that doesn't seem to stop recreational boaters, swimmers and sunbathers from lounging on Lovells' long rocky beach. With facilities for camping and picnicking, Lovells is one of the most popular Harbor Islands destinations. Incidentally, European settlers used the island as a rabbit run, and descendent bunnies are still running this place.

www.bostonharbor islands.org

admission free

🕙 9am-dusk, mid-Apr–mid-Oct

🚢 from Long Wharf

☑ Top Tips

▶ Don't try to visit more than two or three islands in one day: you'll end up spending all your time riding on or waiting for boats.

▶ Check the website for special events, such as live music, outdoor activities and other family programs on Georges and Spectacle Islands.

✗ Take a Break

Georges and Spectacle Islands have snack shacks (open 10am to 5pm) but there is no food or water on the other islands. Pack a picnic!

Understand
Harbor Islands in a Day

Hop on the first ferry at 9am to Georges Island, where you can spend about two hours exploring Fort Warren. After lunch, take the shuttle to Lovells Island to catch some rays on the otherwise empty beach and cool off in the refreshing Atlantic waters. Spend a few hours on Lovells' rocky shores, then take the afternoon shuttle to Grape Island, where you can hunt for wild berries. Take the last shuttle back to Georges Island to catch the 5pm ferry to the mainland.

Bumpkin Island

The beaches at Bumpkin are not the best for swimming, as they are slate and seashell. But there's a network of trails through fields overgrown with wildflowers, leading to the remains of a stone farmhouse and an old hospital. It's one of four islands with camping facilities.

Grape Island

Grape Island is rich with fruity goodness – not grapes, but raspberries, bayberries and elderberries, all growing wild amid the scrubby wooded trails. The wild fruit attracts abundant bird life, making this a great destination for birders, as well as campers.

Peddocks Island

One of the largest Harbor Islands, Peddocks consists of four headlands connected by sandbars. Hiking trails wander through marshes, ponds and coastal environs, and around the remains of Fort Andrews. There are facilities for camping, picnicking and swimming.

Little Brewster Island

Little Brewster is the country's oldest light station and site of the iconic Boston Light. Make reservations for a **tour** (☎617-223-8666; www.bostonharbor islands.org/tour-lighthouse; ⏰10am & 1:30pm Fri-Sun late Jun–mid-Oct; 🚢Fan Pier), departing from Moakley Court-house Dock in the Seaport District. Tours were suspended for construction on Little Brewster in 2014, but are expected to resume in 2015.

Thompson Island

Thompson Island is owned by **Outward Bound** (☎617-328-3900; www. thompsonisland.org; ⏰Sat & Sun Jun-Aug), a nonprofit organization that develops fun and challenging physical adventures. The public can explore its 200-plus acres only on Saturday and Sunday, when it's wonderful for walking, fishing and birding. A dedicated ferry leaves from EDIC Pier in the Seaport District; see the website for details.

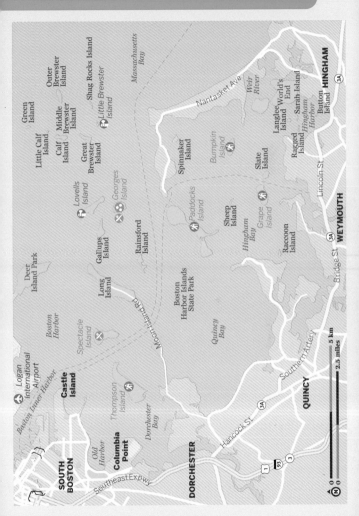

Explore

South End & Chinatown

Chinatown, the Theater District and the Leather District are overlapping areas filled with glitzy theaters, Chinese restaurants and the remnants of Boston's shoe and leather industry (now converted lofts and trendy clubs). Nearby, the South End's Victorian manses have been reclaimed by artists and gay men, who have created a vibrant restaurant and gallery scene in a formerly rough-and-tumble neighborhood.

The Sights in a Day

☀ These four side-by-side neighborhoods do not really contain any traditional 'sights,' but they are home to Boston's lively theater scene, its most hip-hop-happening nightclubs and its best international and contemporary dining. To check it out, head first to the South End for shopping (p88) along Tremont St.

☀ Take lunch at the **South End Buttery** (p79) or **Picco** (p83). In the afternoon, you can explore the galleries in the **SoWa art district** (p78).

☾ For dinner, you'll have to choose between something contemporary and cool in the South End, such as **Coppa** (p82), or something authentically Asian in Chinatown, such as the **Gourmet Dumpling House** (p82). Afterwards, treat yourself to a show in the Theater District or dance the night away at **Underbar** (p85).

For a peek into the local art scene, follow the South End Art Walk (p78).

 Local Life

South End Art Walk (p78)

 Best of Boston

Eating

Gourmet Dumpling House (p82)

Coppa (p82)

Myers & Chang (p82)

Drinking

Beehive (p84)

Fritz (p84)

Club Café (p85)

Entertainment

Cutler Majestic Theatre (p86)

Shubert Theatre (p87)

Shopping

Bobby from Boston (p88)

SoWa Open Market (p88)

Sault New England (p88)

Getting There

🅣 **Metro** The orange line is the most useful, with stops at Chinatown, Back Bay/South End and New England Medical Center.

🚌 **Bus** Good for the South End, the silver line bus runs down Washington St from South Station (SL4) or Downtown Crossing (SL5).

Local Life
South End Art Walk

Boston's edgiest and artiest neighborhood is the South End. The artistic community has moved into the once-barren area south of Washington St (now known as SoWa), converting old warehouses into studios and galleries. For best results, do this walk on a Sunday in summer (May to October) or in the evening on the first Friday of the month (year-round).

1 SoWa Artists Guild

This is the epicenter of the South End art scene, where artists have carved out studios and gallery space from former warehouses and factories on Harrison Ave. **SoWa Artists Guild** (www.sowaartistsguild.com; 450 Harrison Ave, enter Thayer St; SL4 or SL5, New England Medical Center) hosts an **Open Studios** (5-9pm 1st Fri of month) event and **SoWa Sundays** (www.sowasundays.com; 10am-4pm Sun May-Oct) in summer.

2 **Thayer Street Galleries**

There are dozens of venues in the former warehouses at 450 and 460 Harrison Ave (enter from Thayer St). **Bromfield Art Gallery** (www.bromfield gallery.com; 450 Harrison Ave; ⊘noon-5pm Wed-Sat; T New England Medical Center) is a long-running artist-run gallery that features New England artists.

3 **Boston Sculptors Gallery**

Peek into this unusual cooperative gallery, which has been going strong for 20-plus years. Three dozen local artists run the innovative **Boston Sculptors Gallery** (www.bostonsculptors.com; 486 Harrison Ave; ⊘noon-6pm Wed-Sun; T New England Medical Center), dedicated to three-dimensional art of all media.

4 **Ars Libri**

Ring the doorbell: **Ars Libri** (www. arslibri.com; 500 Harrison Ave; ⊘9am-6pm Mon-Fri, 11am-5pm Sat; ☐ SL4 or SL5, T New England Medical Center) is an art bookstore extraordinaire, specializing in rare and out-of-print books. The former warehouse is filled from floor to ceiling with books on all aspects and eras of art, architecture and design. If you love books, and especially books about art, you'll love Ars Libri.

5 **The Gallows**

Turn up to Washington St and into the **Gallows** (www.thegallowsboston.com; 1395 Washington St; ☐ SL4 or SL5, T New England Medical Center). It's hard to say whether it's a restaurant with amazing cocktails and a cozy, crowded, convivial atmosphere; or a bar with irresistible and innovative food. It's a fave among trendy, friendly South Enders.

6 **South End Buttery**

If it's too early for drinks, head up the street to the **South End Buttery** (www.southendbuttery.com; 314 Shawmut Ave; meals $6-10; ⊘6:30am-8pm; ✍ ♿; ☐ SL4 or SL5, T Back Bay) for coffee and cupcakes. A portion of revenue goes to a local animal shelter, coffee drinks feature shade-grown organic beans and packaging materials are made from recycled paper. Now that your conscience is eased, indulge!

7 **Union Park**

Continue up Union Park St to get a glimpse of the charming Victorian rowhouses, clustered around a tree-lined, fountain-filled park. This is South End architecture at its best.

8 **Boston Center for the Arts**

Finish up your walk at this catch-all neighborhood **arts center** (www. bcaonline.org; 539 Tremont St; T Back Bay), which serves as a nexus for small theater productions. Every year, some 20 companies present more than 45 separate productions, ranging from the experimental to the outrageous. You might also catch a concert at the **Community Music Center** (www.cmcb. org; 34 Warren Ave; T Back Bay/South End) or an exhibit opening at the **Mills Gallery** (www.bcaonline.org; 539 Tremont St; ⊘noon-5pm Wed & Sun, to 9pm Thu-Sat; T Back Bay).

Colonial
Theatre

🚇 Boylston

🚇 Chinatown

Essex St

LEATHER
DISTRICT

🚇 South
Station 🚇

E · F · G · H · 1

🚇 15

LaGrange St

Stuart St

12 🍸

8 🍴 4 😣

1 😣

Oxford St

Chinatown
Park

Tufts St

East St

Atlantic Ave

22 🔒

🏛 17

CHINATOWN

😣 7

Surface Rd

Beach St

Utica St

South St

5 · Shawmut Ave

Wang
Theatre

New England 🚇
Medical
Center

Harvard St

Tyler St

Hudson St

Kneeland St

3

Ash St

Harrison Ave

Lincoln St

2

Oak St W

Washington St

US South
Boston
Postal Annex

Pine St

Dorchester Ave

Herald St

Fort Point Channel

3

Harrison Ave

The Boston
Herald

Broadway)

Bass River

Broadway 🚇

Traveler St

4

W Fourth St

W Broadway

93
1

For reviews see

😣 Eating   p82
🍸 Drinking   p84
🏛 Entertainment   p86
🔒 Shopping   p88

18 🔒
Bristol St

Thayer St

19 🔒

Randolph St

Ⓝ 0 _____ 400 m
   0 _____ 0.2 miles

Eating

Gourmet Dumpling House

CHINESE, TAIWANESE $

1 🍽 | Map p80, F1

Xiao long bao. That's all the Chinese you need to know to take advantage of the specialty at the Gourmet Dumpling House (or GDH, as it is fondly called). They are Shanghai soup dumplings, of course, and they are fresh, doughy and delicious. The menu offers plenty of other options, including scrumptious crispy scallion pancakes. (www.gourmetdumpling.com; 52 Beach St; lunch $8, dinner mains $10-15; ⏰11am-1am; ✍; Ⓣ Chinatown)

Q Local Life
Chinatown Market Tour

If you want an insider's perspective, take the **Chinatown Market Tour** (☎617-523-6032; www.bostonfoodtours. com; per person $65; ⏰9:30am-1pm Thu & Sat) and let local chef Jim Becker guide you through the crowded, chaotic streets of Chinatown. There are stops at a produce market, a Chinese bakery, an herbal pharmacy and a traditional teahouse, with plenty of shopping and cooking tips along the way. The tour ends with a dim sum feast.

Coppa

ITALIAN $$$

2 🍽 | Map p80, C5

Ken Oringer and Jamie Bissonette have a knack for recreating dining experiences from around the world with authenticity and innovation. This South End *enoteca* (wine bar) is no exception, serving up *salumi* (cured meats), antipasti, pasta and other delicious Italian small plates. Wash it all down with an Aperol spritz and you might be tricked into thinking you're in Venice. (☎617-391-0902; www.coppaboston.com; 253 Shawmut Ave; small plates $10-22; ⏰noon-10pm Mon-Thu, noon-11pm Fri, 5-11pm Sat, 3-10pm Sun; Ⓢ SL4 or SL5, Ⓣ Back Bay)

Myers & Chang

ASIAN $$

3 🍽 | Map p80, D4

This super-hip Asian spot blends Thai, Chinese and Vietnamese cuisines, which means delicious dumplings, spicy stir-fries and oodles of noodles. The kitchen staff does amazing things with a wok, and the menu of small plates allows you to sample a wide selection of dishes. The vibe is casual but cool, international and independent. (☎617-542-5200; www.myersandchang. com; 1145 Washington St; small plates $10-18; ⏰11:30am-11pm Fri & Sat, to 10pm Sun-Thu; ✍; Ⓢ SL4 or SL5, Ⓣ New England Medical Center)

Gourmet Dumpling House

Xinh Xinh
VIETNAMESE $

4 Map p80, F1

This place wins our award for Boston's favorite *pho* (pronounced 'fuh'), the sometimes exotic, always fragrant and flavorful Vietnamese noodle soup. These hot, hearty meals come in big bowls and warm you from the inside out. The lemongrass tofu is especially recommended, as are the roll-it-yourself spring rolls (work for your food!). (www.xinhxinhboston.com; 7 Beach St; mains $8-12; 10am-10pm; ; Chinatown)

Butcher Shop
FRENCH, ITALIAN $$$

5 Map p80, B4

Only in the South End does the neighborhood butcher shop double as an elegant eatery and wine bar. The cases filled with tantalizing cuts of meat, fresh foie gras and homemade sausages give you a glimpse of the ingredients and provide the decoration at this classy bistro. A nice selection of artisanal wines accompanies the food. (617-423-4800; www.thebutchershopboston.com; 552 Tremont St; petite charcuterie $15, mains $23-40; noon-midnight Mon-Fri, from 11am Sat & Sun; Back Bay)

Picco
PIZZA $$

6 Map p80, C4

The crust of a Picco pizza undergoes a two-day process of cold fermentation before it goes into the oven and then

into your mouth; the result is a thin crust with substantial texture and rich flavor. You can add toppings to create your own pie, or try the specialty 'Alsatian' (sautéed onions, shallots, garlic, sour cream, bacon and Gruyère cheese).
(www.piccorestaurant.com; 513 Tremont St; mains $9-15; ⏱11am-10pm Sun-Thu, to 11pm Fri & Sat; 🛜 🪧 🚻; T Back Bay)

Winsor Dim Sum Cafe

DIM SUM $

7 Map p80, F1

The downside is that there are no pushcarts to choose your food from, as the place is tiny. The upside is that the food is freshly made to order and it is delicious. The shrimp dumplings and steamed pork buns are highly recommended.
(10 Tyler St; items $2-6; ⏱9am-10pm; 🪧; T Chinatown)

My Thai Vegan Café

THAI $

8 🍴 Map p80, F1

This welcoming cafe is tucked into a sunlit, second-story space. It's an animal-free zone – but good enough that meat-eaters will enjoy eating here, too. The menu has a Thai twist, offering noodle soups, dumplings and pad thai. The bubble tea gets raves. Service can be slow, so bring a book.
(3 Beach St; mains $8-12; ⏱11am-10pm; 🪧; T Chinatown)

Drinking

Beehive

JAZZ, COCKTAIL BAR

9 🍸 Map p80, B4

The Beehive has transformed the basement of the Boston Center for the Arts into a 1920s Paris jazz club. This place is more about the scene than the music – which is often provided by students from Berklee College of Music – but the food is good and the vibe is definitely hip. Reservations required if you want a table.
(📞617-423-0069; www.beehiveboston.com; 541 Tremont St; ⏱5pm-1am Mon-Wed, to 2am Thu-Fri, 10am-2am Sat & Sun; T Back Bay)

Fritz

GAY

10 🍸 Map p80, C3

Enjoy a long bar full of chatty men and lots of bottles of booze, all dimly lit by pink Christmas lights that enhance Fritz's atmosphere without it feeling kitschy. It's a comfortable,

low-key spot to watch the boys play ball – or to watch the boys watching the boys playing ball.
(www.fritzboston.com; 26 Chandler St; ⏰noon-2am daily, from 10am Sat & Sun; Ⓣ Back Bay)

Club Café
GAY, CLUB

11 Map p80, B2

This glossy dance club is a mainstay of gay Boston. There is live cabaret in the Napoleon Room five nights a week, while the main dance and lounge area has tea parties, salsa dancing, trivia competitions, karaoke and good old-fashioned dance parties, depending on the night.
(www.clubcafe.com; 209 Columbus Ave; ⏰11am-2am; Ⓣ Back Bay)

Jacob Wirth
BEER HALL

12 Map p80, E1

Boston's second-oldest eatery is this atmospheric Bavarian beer hall. The menu features Wiener schnitzel, sauerbraten, potato pancakes and pork chops, but the highlight is the beer – almost 30 different drafts, including Jake's House Lager and Jake's Special Dark. On Friday nights, Jake hosts a sing-along that rouses the *haus*.
(☎617-338-8586; www.jacobwirth.com; 31-37 Stuart St; sandwiches $8-12, mains $16-22; ⏰11:30am-9:30pm Mon-Thu, to 12:30am Fri & Sat; ♿; Ⓣ Boylston)

Underbar
CLUB

13 Map p80, E2

House music pounds out of the hard-working sound system and reverberates off the walls in this basement club. Unfortunately, the dance floor is small, but if you want to feel the beat – really feel it, because the bass is making your body throb – get down under. 'Hot Mess' Sunday is a crazy, non-stop boozing, cruising gay party.
(www.underbaronline.com; 275 Tremont St; cover $10-20; ⏰10pm-2am Fri-Sun; Ⓣ New England Medical Center)

RISE
CLUB

14 Map p80, C2

The clubs are closing and you still want more – that's when you head over to RISE. The black light and trance music create an otherworldly

Local Life
Delux Café

This delightful **dive bar** (Map p80, B3; ☎617-338-5258; 100 Chandler St; ⏰5pm-1am Mon-Sat; Ⓣ Back Bay) is one of a kind. The small room on the 1st floor of a brownstone comes covered in knotty-pine paneling, artwork from old LPs and Christmas lights. A small TV in the corner plays silent cartoons (not sports), and a noteworthy kitchen serves incredible grilled-cheese sandwiches and inspired comfort food.

atmosphere, where you'll see all kinds of people getting jiggy with it on the dance floor. There is no alcohol; in fact, even a bottle of water is pretty pricey.

(www.riseclub.us; 306 Stuart St; cover $20, students $10; ⏰1-6am Fri & Sat; Ⓣ Arlington)

Entertainment

Cutler Majestic Theatre   OPERA

15 ⭐ Map p80, E1

This beautiful beaux-arts opera house dates to 1903. The performances that take place here are incredibly diverse,

---

Understand
Boston Depicted...

Considering Boston's rich literary tradition and its cinematic architecture, it's no surprise that the city is well represented both in print and on screen.

In Print

▶ *The Scarlet Letter* (Nathaniel Hawthorne; 1850) Hypocrisy and malice in Puritan New England.

▶ *Given Day* (Dennis Lehane; 2008) Historical novel follows two families through the turbulence of post-WWI Boston.

▶ *Interpreter of Maladies* (Jhumpa Lahiri; 1999) Pulitzer Prize–winner on the challenges of migration and multiculturalism.

▶ *The Friends of Eddie Coyle* (George Higgins; 1972) A crime novel with a crash course in the Boston dialect.

▶ *Infinite Jest* (David Foster Wallace; 1996) A thousand-page tome that's at once philosophical and satirical.

On Screen

▶ *The Verdict* (1982) Paul Newman stars as a Boston lawyer.

▶ *Good Will Hunting* (1997) The film that put South Boston on the map.

▶ *Next Stop Wonderland* (1997) Heartwarming independent film with a bossa nova soundtrack.

▶ *The Departed* (2006) Suspense-filled mob movie that won Best Picture.

▶ *The Social Network* (2010) Fictionalized drama of the founding of Facebook.

LOU JONES/GETTY IMAGES ©

Festival performer, Chinatown

including shows by **Opera Boston** (www.operaboston.org; 219 Tremont St, Cutler Majestic box office; tickets $24-99; ⊤ Boylston), seasonal celebrations such as the popular Celtic Christmas Sojourn, dance events such as the Flamenco Festival or Tango Stories, comedy, music and more. (☎617-824-8000; www.maj.org; 219 Tremont St; ⊤ Boylston)

Shubert Theatre   OPERA

 16 Map p80, E2

With 1600 seats, the Shubert is smaller and more intimate than some of the other Theater District venues, thus earning it the moniker the 'Little Princess' of the Theater District. The Shubert is the place to see the **Boston Lyric Opera** (www.blo.org; tickets $33-112) and other musical theater. (www.citicenter.org; 265 Tremont St; ⊤ Boylston)

Wilbur Theatre   COMEDY

17 Map p80, E1

The colonial Wilbur Theatre dates to 1914, and over the years has hosted many prominent theatrical productions. These days it's Boston's premier comedy club. Once known as the Comedy Connection, this long-running operation has hosted the likes of Chris Rock, Rosie O'Donnell and other nationally known cut-ups. (www.thewilburtheatre.com; 246 Tremont St; tickets $20-50; ⊤ Boylston)

Shopping

Bobby From Boston
CLOTHING, VINTAGE

18 Map p80, E5

Bobby is one of Boston's coolest cats. Men from all over the greater Boston area come to the South End to peruse Bobby's amazing selection of classic clothing from another era. This is stuff that your grandfather wore – if he was a very stylish man.

(19 Thayer St; ☺noon-6pm Mon-Sat; ⬛SL4 or SL5, Ⓣ New England Medical Center)

✓ Top Tip

South End on Sunday

Summer Sundays are lively in the South End, which hosts **SoWa Sundays** (p78) from May to October. Three different markets fill the art district's parking lots: the **SoWa Open Market** (p88) for arts and crafts; **SoWa Vintage Market** (Map p80, E5; www.sowavintagemarket. com; ☺10am-4pm Sun, 5-9pm first Fri; ⬛SL4 or SL5, Ⓣ New England Medical Center) for antiques and treasures; and the **SoWa Farmers Market** (Map p80, D5; www.newenglandopenmarkets.com; 500 Harrison Ave; ☺10am-4pm Sun May-Oct; ⬛SL4 or SL5, Ⓣ New England Medical Center) for all your fresh produce needs.

SoWa Open Market
HANDICRAFTS, MARKET

19 Map p80, E5

Part flea market and part artists' market, this weekly outdoor event is a fabulous opportunity for strolling and shopping, with more than a hundred vendors set up under white tents. It's never the same two weeks in a row, but there's always plenty of arts and crafts, as well as edgier art, vintage clothing, jewelry, local farm produce and homemade sweets.

(www.newenglandopenmarkets.com; 460 Harrison Ave; ☺10am-4pm Sun May-Oct; ⬛SL4 or SL5, Ⓣ New England Medical Center)

Sault New England
CLOTHING, GIFTS

20 Map p80, R4

Blending prepster and hipster, rustic and chic, this little basement boutique packs in a lot of intriguing stuff. The eclectic mix of merchandise runs the gamut from new and vintage clothing to coffee-table books and homemade terrariums. A New England theme runs through the store, with nods to the Kennedys, *Jaws,* and LL Bean.

(www.saultne.com; 577 Tremont St; ☺11am-7pm Tue-Sun; Ⓣ Back Bay)

Motley
CLOTHING, GIFTS

21 Map p80, A5

This little shoebox of a store lives up to its name, offering a motley array of hip clothing, funny books and novelty gift items. The ever-changing product line includes comfy, clever T-shirts

Calamus Bookstore

and true-blue vintage Boston sports-fan gear. You absolutely do not need anything on offer here, but you will absolutely find something that you *have* to own.
(www.shopmotley.com; 623 Tremont St; T Back Bay)

Calamus Bookstore   BOOKS

22 🔒 Map p80, H1

The Greek deity Calamus was trans-formed with grief into a reed when his lover drowned. The character inspired Walt Whitman's 'Calamus' poems, which celebrate gay love. And now, he has inspired Boston's biggest and best GLBT bookstore. With a full calendar of author talks and art exhibitions, as well as a regular electronic newsletter, Calamus is not just a bookstore but also a commu-nity center.
(www.calamusbooks.com; 92 South St; ⊙9am-7pm Mon-Sat, noon-6pm Sun; T South Station)

Explore

Back Bay

Back Bay includes the city's most fashionable window-shopping, latte-drinking and people-watching area – found on Newbury St – as well as its most elegant architecture around Copley Sq. Once an uninhabitable tidal flat (thus the name), in the late 19th century the area was filled in to create a residential neighborhood of magnificent Victorian brownstones and high-minded civic plazas.

The Sights in a Day

☀️ Start your day with a coffee and scone from **Flour** (p101). Then walk a few blocks to Copley Sq, which offers the best of Back Bay architecture. Peek into **Trinity Church** (p94) to marvel at the stained-glass windows and multi-tiered murals. Then take a self-guided tour of the masterworks at the **Boston Public Library** (p92). Treat yourself to lunch at the library's lovely restaurant, **Courtyard** (p100).

☀️ After admiring the architecture and browsing the books, you are perfectly placed for an afternoon of window-shopping and gallery-hopping along swanky **Newbury St** (p106). Get a different perspective on the city at the **Prudential Center Skywalk Observatory** (p100) – or get a different perspective on the world at the **Mapparium** (p100).

🌙 Take your pick from the neighborhood's fine venues for dinner, followed by live music at the **Red Room @ Cafe 939** (p105).

For a day discovering local fashion and design, take the Back Bay Fashion Walk (p96).

Top Sights

Boston Public Library (p92)

Trinity Church (p94)

Local Life

Back Bay Fashion Walk (p96)

Best of Boston

Eating

The Courtyard (p100)

Bistro du Midi (p101)

Drinking

Bukowski Tavern (p104)

Top of the Hub (p104)

Entertainment

Red Room @ Café 939 (p105)

Shopping

Lunarik Fashions (p97)

Ball & Buck (p97)

Getting There

🚇 **Metro** The main branch of the green line runs along Boylston St, with stops at Arlington near the Public Garden, Copley at Copley Sq and Hynes at Mass Ave. The green E-line branch follows Huntington Ave to Prudential and Symphony.

🚇 **Metro** The orange-line stop Back Bay/South End is on the border between these two neighborhoods.

Top Sights
Boston Public Library

Dating from 1852, the esteemed Boston Public Library (BPL) was built as a 'shrine of letters,' lending credence to Boston's reputation as the 'Athens of America.' The old McKim building is notable for its magnificent facade (inspired by Italian Renaissance *palazzi*) and exquisite interior art. Before entering, note Mora and Saint-Gaudens' carving of Minerva, Roman goddess of wisdom, on the central keystone on the facade. Then proceed through Daniel Chester French's enormous bronze doorways, flanked by iron gates and lanterns.

👁 Map p98, E3

www.bpl.org

700 Boylston St

🕐 9am-9pm Mon-Thu, to 5pm Fri & Sat year-round, plus 1-5pm Sun Oct-May

🚊 Copley

Boston Public Library interior

Don't Miss

Puvis de Chavannes Gallery

The main marble staircase leads past Pierre Puvis de Chavannes' inspirational murals, depicting poetry, philosophy, history and science, which he considered 'the four great expressions of the human mind.' Upstairs, at the entrance to Bates Hall, is another Puvis de Chavannes mural, with the nine muses from Greek mythology honoring the Genius of the Enlightenment.

Bates Hall

The staircase terminates at Bates Hall, where even mundane musings are elevated by the barrel-vaulted, 50ft-high coffered ceiling. In 1852, Joshua Bates was the BPL's original benefactor, who stipulated that 'the building shall be...an ornament to the city, that there shall be a room for 100 to 150 persons to sit at reading-tables, [and] that it be perfectly free to all.'

Abbey Room

The Abbey Room is among the library's most sumptuous, with its oak wainscoting, marble flooring and elaborate fireplace. The room is named for the author of the 1895 murals, which recount Sir Galahad's quest for the Holy Grail.

Sargent Gallery

On the 3rd floor is the library's pièce de résistance: John Singer Sargent's unfinished mural series, *The Triumph of Religion*. They trace the history of Western religion, from paganism to Judaism to Christianity. A final painting was intended for the vacant space above the stairwell, but the mural was never completed, due in part to strong criticism from the Jewish community.

☑ Top Tips

▶ The BPL offers free guided art and architecture tours, leaving from the entrance hall at 2pm Sunday and Monday, 6pm on Tuesday and Thursday, and 11am on Wednesday, Friday and Saturday.

▶ The special collections hold countless treasures, including John Adams' personal library. Check the BPL website for details of exhibits showcasing the highlights, as well as a schedule of free events, from author talks to musical performances.

▶ Don't leave without taking a moment of contemplation in the peaceful Italianate courtyard.

✗ Take a Break

Grab a coffee or snack at the on-site **Map Room Cafe** (www.thecateredaffair.com; breakfast & sandwiches $5-8; ⏲9am-5pm Mon-Fri; 🛜🖥). For something more formal, dine at the exquisite **Courtyard** (p100).

Top Sights
Trinity Church

A masterpiece of American architecture, Trinity Church is the country's ultimate example of Richardsonian Romanesque. The granite exterior, with a massive portico and side cloister, uses sandstone in colorful patterns. The interior is an awe-striking array of vibrant murals and stained glass, most by artist John LaFarge, who cooperated closely with architect Henry Hobson Richardson to create an integrated composition of shapes, colors and textures.

👁 Map p98, E3

www.trinitychurchboston.org

206 Clarendon St

adult/child/senior & student $7/free/5

🕐 10am-3:30pm Mon-Fri, 9am-4pm Sat, 1-5pm Sun

Ⓣ Copley

Don't Miss

LaFarge Murals
The walls of the great central tower are covered by two tiers of murals, soaring more than 100ft high. Prior to this commission, LaFarge did not have experience with mural painting on this scale. The result – thousands of square feet of exquisite, jewel-toned encaustic paintings – established his authority as the father of the American mural movement.

Stained-Glass Windows
The 33 stained-glass windows – mostly executed by different glass workshops – represent diverse styles. The original windows from 1877 and 1878 are the traditional European designs, completed by premier English workshops. Several later examples represent the English Arts & Crafts movement, while the ornate French windows were designed by Parisian artist Achille François Oudinot.

LaFarge Windows
The jewels of the church are the work of LaFarge, distinctive for their use of layered opalescent glass, resulting in an unprecedented richness of shades and dimensions. LaFarge's first commission was *Christ in Majesty,* the spectacular three-panel clerestory window at the western end that is now considered one of the USA's finest examples of stained-glass art.

Architecture
The footprint of Trinity Church is a Greek cross, with chancel, nave and transepts surrounding the central square. The wide-open interior was a radical departure from traditional Episcopal architecture, but it embodies the democratic spirit of the congregation in the 1870s.

☑ Top Tips
▶ Free architectural tours are offered following Sunday service at 11:15am. Additional tours are offered daily throughout the week (times vary).

▶ Free concerts on the impressive pipe organ are held on Fridays at 12:15pm.

▶ Snap a photo from Clarendon St to catch the exquisite church reflected in the facade of the nearby John Hancock Tower.

✕ Take a Break
Stop for sustenance at **Flour** (p101), which gets rave reviews for its rich coffee, fresh-made scones and pastries, and delectable, satisfying soups and sandwiches.

Local Life
Back Bay Fashion Walk

Welcome to designer row. On New-bury St, you'll have no problem procuring Diesel jeans, a Fendi bag or an Armani suit. But this is also the place to see how local design-ers are working to put Boston on the map *à la mode*.

❶ School of Fashion Design

Up-and-coming local talents hone their skills and experiment with their ideas at the **School of Fashion Design** (www.schooloffashiondesign.org; 136 Newbury St; T Copley), Boston's only educational institution focusing exclusively on fashion. Check out the 'fashion art space' at the on-site A Gallery, which hosts exhibits exploring the intersec-tion of fashion, art and design.

❷ Ball & Buck

The hunter logo at **Ball & Buck** (www.ballandbuck.com; 144 Newbury St; ⏰11am-8pm; Ⓣ Copley) is indicative of this brand's target market – manly men who look good in camouflage and love America. Both sophisticated and sporty, these attractive, durable duds are meant to be worn in the woods or on the Boston city streets. Made in the US.

❸ Society of Arts & Crafts

Since 1897, this prestigious nonprofit **gallery** (www.societyofcrafts.org; 175 Newbury St; ⏰10am-6pm Tue-Sat; Ⓣ Copley) has been showcasing the innovative work of emerging and established artists and designers. The collection changes constantly, but you'll find weaving, leather, ceramics, glassware and furniture, all hand-crafted by society members.

❹ Daniela Corte

Born and raised in Buenos Aires, Daniela Corte attended the Boston School of Fashion Design before launching her own line and opening this sleek **boutique** (www.danielacorte.com; 211 Newbury St; ⏰11am-7pm Mon-Sat; Ⓣ Copley) on Newbury St. Browse her collection of silky tops, fun dresses and skin-hugging leggings, all of which are made in the upstairs studio.

❺ Tobey Grey

You'll find classy clothes by nationally-known designers at this fabulous boutique, but the house collection at **Tobey Grey** (218 Newbury St; ⏰11am-7pm Mon-Sat, to 6pm Sun; Ⓣ Copley) is more affordable and still scores major style points. Although there's no shortage of exquisite tops and sharp dresses, the most popular items are the super-soft, ultra-flattering tees and tanks. Every girl can use a few of these!

❻ Sikara & Co

Mousumi travels the world to seek inspiration for the amazing 'modern fusion jewelry' you'll find in **Sikara & Co** (www.sikara.com; 250 Newbury St; ⏰10am-7pm Mon-Sat, 11am-6pm Sun; Ⓣ Hynes). From her native India to countries the world over, she works with designers to incorporate semi-precious stones, precious metals and exotic design elements into these miniature masterpieces. Inspiration through travel – that's a concept we can get behind!

❼ Lunarik Fashions

Like a modern woman's handbag, **Lunarik** (279 Newbury St; ⏰11am-7pm Mon-Fri, 10am-8pm Sat, noon-6pm Sun; Ⓣ Hynes) is packed with useful stuff, much of it by local designers. Look for whimsical collage-covered pieces by Jenn Sherr, beautiful hand-crafted jewelry by Dasken Designs, and the best-selling, richly colored leather handbags by Saya Cullinan.

Charles River

Harvard Bridge

2A

Charles River Bike Path

Storrow Dr

Back St

Beacon St

Marlborough St

Storrow Dr

Massachusetts Ave

Charlesgate Overpass

Hereford St

Gloucester St

Fairfield St

2

Commonwealth Ave

BACK BAY

Exeter St

🚇 Kenmore

Newbury St

18 15

19

10

6

8

9

Ring Rd

Boylston St

16 20

Massachusetts Turnpike

Ipswich St

Hynes

13

Hynes Convention Center

Prudential Center Skywalk Observatory

1

90

Boylston St

11

14

Scotia St

Dalton St

Belvidere St

Haviland St

St Germain St

🚇 Prudential

Community Victory Gardens

Muddy River

Norway St

Edgerly Rd

Mary Baker Eddy Library & Mapparium

2

FENWAY

Burbank St

Huntington Ave

St Botolph St

Claremont St

Durham

Westland Ave

3

Christian Science Church

Agassiz Rd

Hemenway St

Symphony Rd

Gainsborough St

Symphony Hall

Cumberland St

Columbus Ave

🚇 Symphony

Kelleher Rose Garden

The Fenway

St Stephens St

Massachusetts Avenue

E

F

G Byron St

H

Beacon St

The Esplanade

Public Garden

Boston Common

Storrow Dr

Arlington St

Charles St

28

Berkeley St

Clarendon St

Dartmouth St

Commonwealth Ave

The Lagoon

Four Seasons Hotel

Boylston St

Boylston

Tremont St

Newbury St

7

2

5

Boylston St

Arlington

Copley

Boylston St

Providence St

St James Ave

Park Plaza

Statler Park

THEATER DISTRICT

Stuart St

Boston Public Library

12

Copley Square

Trinity Church

Trinity Pl

John Hancock Tower

Stuart St

Columbus Ave

Church St

Melrose St

Fayette St

Charles St S

Tremont St

New England Medical Center

Blagden St

Isabella St

Cortes St

Tremont St

CHINATOWN

4

Massachusetts Turnpike

Marginal Rd

90

Back Bay

Chandler St

Berkeley St

Herald St

Paul Pl

Tent City

Yarmouth St

W Canton St

Lawrence St

Appleton St

Clarendon St

Gray St

Tremont St

Shawmut Ave

Washington St

Holyoke St

Dartmouth St

Warren Ave

SOUTH END

Milford St

Hanson St

Columbus Square

W Brookline St

Pembroke St

W Newton St

Rutland Sq

Montgomery St

Tremont St

Upton St

Drapers La

W Dedham St

Shawmut Ave

ROXBURY

For reviews see	
◉ Top Sights	p92
◉ Sights	p100
✕ Eating	p100
◒ Drinking	p104
✪ Entertainment	p105
⬟ Shopping	p106

0 400 m
0 0.2 miles

Sights

Prudential Center Skywalk Observatory

LOOKOUT

1 ◉ Map p98, D4

Technically called the Shops at Prudential Center, this landmark Boston building is not much more than a fancy shopping mall, but it does provide a bird's-eye view of Boston from its 50th-floor skywalk. Completely enclosed by glass, the skywalk offers spectacular 360-degree views of Boston and Cambridge, accompanied by an entertaining audio tour (with a special version catering to kids). (www.prudentialcenter.com; 800 Boylston St; adult/child/senior & student $16/11/13; ⊙10am-10pm Mar-Oct, to 8pm Nov-Feb; P ♿; T Prudential)

Mary Baker Eddy Library & Mapparium

LIBRARY

2 ◉ Map p98, C4

The Mary Baker Eddy Library houses one of Boston's hidden treasures, the intriguing Mapparium – a room-size, stained-glass globe that visitors walk through on a glass bridge. It was created in 1935, which is reflected in the globe's geopolitical boundaries. The acoustics, which surprised even the designer, allow everyone in the room to hear even the tiniest whisper. (www.marybakereddylibrary.org; 200 Massachusetts Ave; adult/child/senior & student $6/free/4; ⊙10am-4pm Tue-Sun; ♿; T Symphony)

Christian Science Church

CHURCH

3 ◉ Map p98, C4

Known to adherents as the 'Mother Church,' this is the international home base for the Church of Christ, Scientist (Christian Science), founded by Mary Baker Eddy in 1866. Tour the grand, classical-revival basilica, which can seat 3000 worshippers; listen to the 14,000-pipe organ; and linger on the expansive plaza with its 670ft-long reflecting pool. (www.christianscience.com; 175 Huntington Ave; ⊙noon-4pm Tue, 1-4pm Wed, noon-5pm Thu-Sat, 11am-3pm Sun, service 10am Sun; T Symphony)

Eating

Courtyard

MODERN AMERICAN $$

The perfect destination for an elegant luncheon with artfully prepared food is – believe it or not – the Boston Public Library (see ◉ Map p98, E3). Overlooking the beautiful Italianate courtyard, this grown-up restaurant serves seasonal, innovative and exotic dishes (along with a few standards). The only downside is the lack of alcohol, but we understand the concern about drinking and reading. (www.thecateredaffair.com; 700 Boylston St; mains $12-17; ⊙lunch Mon-Fri; ♪; T Copley)

NANCY LOUIE/GETTY IMAGES ©

Boston skyline showing the Prudential Center and John Hancock Tower

Flour

BAKERY **$**

4 Map p98, F3

Flour implores patrons to 'make life sweeter...eat dessert first!' It's hard to resist at this pastry-lover's paradise. But dessert is not all: sandwiches, soups, salads and pizzas are also available. And just to prove there is something for everybody, Flour sells housemade dog biscuits for your canine friend.

(www.flourbakery.com; 131 Clarendon St; mains $5-10; ⊙7am-8pm Mon-Fri, 8am-6pm Sat, 9am-5pm Sun; 🛜 🖉 🐾; T Back Bay/ South End)

Bistro du Midi

FRENCH **$$**

5 Map p98, G2

The upstairs dining room is exquisite, but the downstairs cafe exudes warmth and camaraderie, inviting casual callers to linger over wine and snacks. In either setting, the Provençal fare is artfully presented and simply delicious. Reservations are required for dinner upstairs, but drop-ins are welcome at the cafe all day.

(📞617-426-7878; www.bistrodumidi.com; 272 Boylston St; mains $12-24; ⊙lunch & dinner; T Arlington)

Understand

Boston Marathon

Patriots Day – officially celebrated on the third Monday in April – means more than Paul Revere's ride and 'the shot heard 'round the world' (p38). Since 1897, Patriots Day also means the **Boston Marathon** (www.baa.org). Fifteen people ran that first race (only 10 finished); in 2014, a record-breaking 36,000 people were registered to run.

Route

The 26-mile race starts in rural Hopkinton, MA, and winds its way through the western suburbs to Boston. Some of the marathon's most dramatic moments occur between mile 20 and 21, when the aptly named Heartbreak Hill rises a steep 80ft. It's all downhill from there.

Runners cruise up Beacon St, through Kenmore Sq, down 'Comm Ave' (Commonwealth Ave), over to Boylston St, and into a triumphant finish at Copley Sq. This final mile is among the most exciting places to be a spectator.

Marathon Celebrities

The most infamous participant (loosely defined) is Rosie Ruiz, who in 1980 seemingly emerged from nowhere to win the women's division. In fact, she *did* emerge from nowhere, and had actually skipped most of the race. She was disqualified, but remains a marathon legend.

Modern marathon celebrities include **Rick and Dick Hoyt** (www.teamhoyt.com), a father-son team. Rick suffers from cerebral palsy, but his father was determined to give his son the chance to purse his passions, including sports. With Dick pushing his son in a wheelchair, they have completed the Boston Marathon 30 times.

Marathon Bombings

In 2013, the nation (and the world) turned their eyes to Boston when two bombs exploded near the finish line of the Boston Marathon, killing three and injuring hundreds. Several days later, an MIT police officer was shot dead and the entire city was locked down, as Boston became a battle-ground for the War on Terror. The tragedy was devastating, but Boston can claim countless heroes, especially the many victims who have inspired others with their courage and fortitude throughout their recoveries.

Piattini

ITALIAN $$

6 Map p98, D3

If you have trouble deciding what to order, Piattini can help. The name means 'small plates,' so you don't have to choose just one. The list of wines by the glass is extensive, each accompanied by tasting notes and fun facts. This intimate *enoteca* (wine bar) is a delightful setting for sampling the flavors of Italy, and you might just learn something while you're there. (www.piattini.com; 226 Newbury St; lunch $8-15, dinner $18-24; ⊙lunch Mon-Fri, dinner daily; ⌨; ⛆Copley)

Parish Café

SANDWICHES $$

7 Map p98, F2

Sample the creations of Boston's most famous chefs without exhausting your expense account. The menu at Parish features a rotating roster of salads and sandwiches, each designed by a local celebrity chef, including Lydia Shire, Ken Oringer and Barbara Lynch. (www.parishcafe.com; 361 Boylston St; sandwiches $12-15; ⊙noon-2am; ⌨; ⛆Arlington)

Atlantic Fish Co

SEAFOOD $$

8 Map p98, D3

New England clam chowder in a bread bowl. For a perfect lunch at Atlantic Fish Co, that's all you need to know. For the nonbelievers, we will add Maine lobster pot pie, lobster ravioli and jumbo lump crabcakes.

There's more, of course, and the menu is printed up daily to showcase the freshest ingredients. Enjoy it in the seafaring dining room or the flower-filled sidewalk patio. (www.atlanticfishco.com; 761 Boylston St; lunch $12-22, dinner $20-24; ⊙lunch & dinner; ⛆Copley)

L'Espalier

FRENCH $$$

9 Map p98, D3

This tried-and-true favorite remains the crème de la crème of Boston's culinary scene, thanks to impeccable service and a variety of prix-fixe and tasting menus. The menus change daily, but they usually include a

Local Life

Charles River Esplanade

Perfect for picnic lunches and summertime lounging, this **riverside park** (Map p98, C2, D1; www.esplanade-association.org; **T**Charles/MGH or Kenmore) is Boston's backyard. Designed by Frederick Law Olmsted, the Esplanade stretches almost 3 miles along the Boston shore of the Charles River, from the Museum of Science to BU (Boston University) Bridge. Paths along the river are ideal for bicycling, jogging or walking.

degustation of caviar, a degustation of seasonal vegetables and recommended wine pairings. (☎617-262-3023; www.lespalier.com; 774 Boylston St; lunch mains $25, dinner prix fixe $90-110; ☺lunch & dinner Mon-Sat; **T**Prudential)

Drinking

Wired Puppy   CAFE

10 ☕ Map p98, D3

Delicious organic coffee, a welcoming atmosphere and free wifi or computer use. What more do you need? (www.wiredpuppy.com; 250 Newbury St; ☺6:30am-7:30pm; 🛜; **T**Hynes)

Bukowski Tavern   DIVE BAR

11 ☕ Map p98, C3

This sweet bar lies inside a parking garage next to the canyon of the Mass Pike (the local name for the Massachusettes Turnpike). Expect sticky wooden tables, loud rock, lots of black hoodies, a dozen different burgers and dogs and more than 100 kinds of beer. 'In God we trust; all others pay cash.' (www.bukowskitavern.net; 50 Dalton St; ☺11am-2am; **T**Hynes)

Top of the Hub   BAR

Yes, it's touristy. And overpriced. And a little bit snooty. But the head-spinning city view makes it worthwhile to ride the elevator up to the 52nd floor of the Prudential Center (see 1 Map p98, D4). Come for spectacular sunset drinks and stay for free live jazz. Beware the $24 per person minimum after 8pm. (☎617-536-1775; www.topofthehub.net; 800 Boylston St; ☺11:30am-1am; 🛜; **T**Prudential)

Storyville   CLUB

12 ☕ Map p98, E3

The legendary Storyville jazz club occupied this same spot in the 1940s, when it hosted the likes of Dave Brubeck and Billie Holiday (who even recorded an album here). The contemporary nightclub recalls that era with its loungey atmosphere and sexy, New Orleans–inspired vibe.

Harry Belafonte tribute concert at Berklee Performance Center

(www.storyvilleboston.com; 90 Exeter St; ⏰10pm-2am Wed-Thu, 7pm-2am Fri & Sat; T Copley)

Entertainment

Red Room @ Café 939   LIVE MUSIC

13 ⭐ Map p98, C3

Run by students from the Berklee College of Music, the Red Room @ 939 is emerging as one of Boston's best music venues. The place has an excellent sound system and a baby grand piano; most importantly, it books interesting, eclectic up-and-coming musicians. This is where you'll see that band that's about to make it big.

(www.cafe939.com; 939 Boylston St; T Hynes)

Berklee Performance Center   BLUES, JAZZ

14 ⭐ Map p98, C4

For high-energy jazz recitals, smoky-throated vocalists and new age electronica, the performance hall at this notable music college hosts a wide variety of performers. Depending on the night, you'll hear student recitals, invited musicians, instructors or the Ultra Sonic Rock Orchestra. (www.berkleebpc.com; 136 Massachusetts Ave; $8-45; T Hynes)

Shopping

Life is Good
CLOTHING, GIFTS

15 🔒 Map p98, C3

Life *is* good for this locally designed brand of T-shirts, backpacks and other gear. Styles depict the fun-loving stick figure Jake engaged in guitar playing, dog walking, coffee drinking, mountain climbing and just about every other good-vibe diversion you might enjoy. Jake's activity may vary, but his 'life is good' theme is constant. (www.lifeisgood.com; 285 Newbury St; ⏱10am-6pm Mon-Sat, 11am-6pm Sun; Ⓣ Hynes)

Converse
SHOES, CLOTHING

16 🔒 Map p98, C3

Converse started making shoes right up the road in Malden, MA, way back in 1908. Chuck Taylor joined

Local Life
Trident Booksellers

Is this highbrow hangout a **bookstore** (Map p98, C3; www.trident bookscafe.com; 338 Newbury St; ⏱9am-midnight; 📶; Ⓣ Hynes) with an amazingly eclectic menu or a cafe with a super selection of reading material? The collection of books is wide but leans toward political and New Age themes. The food menu is equally varied, ranging from the comforting (muffins, soups, smoothies) to the daring (spinach arancini, Tibetan dumplings).

the 'team' in the 1920s and the rest is history. This retail store has an incredible selection of sneakers, as well as a customization center where you can design your own. (www.converse.com; 348 Newbury St; ⏱10am-7pm, to 8pm Sat, 11am-6pm Sun; Ⓣ Hynes)

Marathon Sports
SPORTS

17 🔒 Map p98, E3

Specializing in running gear, this place could not have a better location: it overlooks the finish line of the Boston Marathon. It's known for attentive customer service, as staff work hard to make sure you are getting a shoe that fits. Besides the latest styles and technologies, Marathon also carries a line of retro style running shoes. (www.marathonsports.com; 671 Boylston St; ⏱10:30am-7:30pm Mon-Fri, 10am-6pm Sat, noon-6pm Sun; Ⓣ Copley)

Ibex
CLOTHING

18 🔒 Map p98, C3

Based in snowy, cold Vermont, Ibex makes outdoor clothing from soft, warm, breathable merino wool. It's not the itchy stuff you remember – this wool is plush and pleasurable, thanks to the fineness of the fiber. Categorized as base layer, midlayer or outerlayer, the clothing is guaranteed to keep you cozy, even through the coldest, snowiest Vermont winter. Bonus: it looks good, too. (www.ibex.com; 303 Newbury St; ⏱10am-7pm Mon-Sat, 11am-6pm Sun; Ⓣ Hynes)

Fairy Shop
GIFTS

19 🔒 Map p98, C3

It's a shop that's dedicated to selling fairies – yes, we mean like Tinker Bell – in every shape and size imaginable, as well as maidens, mermaids, sprites and unicorns. That little gnome from the French film *Amélie* is here too, many times over. So if you'd rather be 'chillin' with your gnomies,' here's where you can do it.
(www.thefairyshop.com; 272 Newbury St; ⏱variable; enquire before visiting; 🇹Hynes)

Newbury Comics
MUSIC

20 🔒 Map p98, C3

Any outlet of this local chain is usually jam-packed with teenagers clad in black and sporting multiple piercings. Apparently these kids know where to find cheap CDs and DVDs. The newest alt-rock albums and the latest movies are on sale here, along with comic books, rock posters and other silly gags. No wonder everyone is having such a wicked good time.
(www.newburycomics.com; 332 Newbury St; ⏱10am-10pm Mon-Fri, to 11pm Sat, 11am-8pm Sun; 🇹Hynes)

Explore

Kenmore Square & Fenway

Kenmore Sq and Fenway are home to Boston's most beloved cultural institutions. The neighborhoods attract club-goers and baseball fans to the streets surrounding Fenway Park, as well as art lovers and culture vultures to the artistic institutions along the Avenue of the Arts (aka Huntington Ave).

The Sights in a Day

☼ Decisions, decisions. You'll want to spend at least part of your day admiring the world-class artwork here in the Fenway, but you're going to have to decide which museum to patronize. It's easy to spend the entire day browsing the Art of the Americas wing, the impressionist and post-impressionist paintings, and the ancient art at the **Museum of Fine Arts** (p110). Or, you can spend a few hours in a more intimate art setting, studying the Italian Renaissance and Dutch Golden Age paintings at the **Isabella Stewart Gardner Museum** (p112).

☼ 'Mrs Jack' Gardner was a Red Sox fan – if you are too, head over to **Fenway Park** (p114) for a tour of America's oldest ballpark.

☾ You have another tough choice for the evening. Plan ahead to get tickets to hear the **Boston Symphony Orchestra** (p118) or to see the **Red Sox** (p119) play at home. Otherwise, indulge in dinner at **Island Creek Oyster Bar** (p117), followed by drinks at the **Hawthorne** (p118).

◉ Top Sights

Museum of Fine Arts (p110)

Isabella Stewart Gardner Museum (p112)

Fenway Park (p114)

♥ Best of Boston

Eating

El Pelon (p117)

Island Creek Oyster Bar (p117)

Drinking

Bleacher Bar (p118)

Hawthorne (p118)

Entertainment

Boston Symphony Orchestra (p118)

Church (p118)

House of Blues (p119)

Huntington Theatre Company (p119)

Getting There

Ⓜ **Metro** To reach Kenmore Sq or Fenway Park, take any of the green-line trains except the E-line to Kenmore T station.

Ⓜ **Metro** The E-line runs along Huntington Ave to Symphony Hall and the Museum of Fine Arts.

Top Sights
Museum of Fine Arts

The Museum of Fine Arts is Boston's premier venue for showcasing art by local, national and international artists. The museum's holdings encompass all eras, from the ancient world to contemporary times, and all areas of the globe, making it truly encyclopedic in scope. With the recent opening of new wings dedicated to the Art of the Americas and to contemporary art, the museum has significantly increased its exhibition space and broadened its focus, contributing to Boston's emergence as an art center in the 21st century.

◉ Map p116, C4

www.mfa.org

465 Huntington Ave

adult/child/senior & student $22/10/20

🕙10am-5pm Sat-Tue, to 10pm Wed-Fri

Ⓣ Museum or Ruggles

Don't Miss

Art of the Americas

On the 2nd level is an entire gallery is dedicated to John Singer Sargent, including his iconic painting *The Daughters of Edward Darley Boit*. Several highlights in the American impressionism galleries include pieces by Mary Cassat, and the perennial local favorite, *Boston Common at Twilight* by Childe Hassam.

20th-Century European Art

The highlights of the European exhibit are the impressionists and post-impressionists, with masterpieces by Degas, Gauguin, Renoir and Van Gogh, as well as the largest collection of Monets outside Paris. Take a moment to ponder Gauguin's large-scale painting *Where Do We Come From?*

Buddhist Temple

Dimly lit and decorated with Buddhist statues, this room is a serene place to regroup before investigating the extensive collection of Asian art.

Egyptian Galleries

In the first half of the 20th century, the MFA and Harvard University cooperated to excavate tombs and temples surrounding the Giza Pyramids, bringing back thousands of artifacts that are now on display. Look for two rooms of mummies, as well as intriguing pottery and statuary.

Linde Family Wing for Contemporary Art

The recent renovation of the west wing – originally designed by IM Pei – has nearly tripled the exhibition space for contemporary art, with galleries dedicated to video, multimedia art and decorative arts. The darling of museum patrons is *Black River*, a fantastic woven tapestry of discarded bottle caps by Ghanaian artist El Anatsui.

☑ Top Tips

▶ You can rent a guided multimedia tour (adult/child $6/4), in one of seven languages which uses video, audio and animation to provide extra insight on the museum's highlights.

▶ Children under the age of 17 are admitted free after 3pm on weekdays and all day on weekends.

▶ Before jumping into the collections, stop to admire the murals in the rotunda and above the main staircase, all painted by John Singer Sargent.

✕ Take a Break

The Linde wing features upscale dining at the restaurant **Bravo** (⊙11:30am-3pm daily, 5:30-8:30pm Wed-Fri; Ⓣ Museum), as well as a cafe and cafeteria. In the Shapiro Courtyard, sample Ken Oringer's menu of modern American cuisine at the **New American Café** (⊙10am-4pm Sat-Tue, to 8pm Wed-Fri; Ⓣ Museum).

Top Sights
Isabella Stewart Gardner Museum

The magnificent Venetian-style *palazzo* that houses this museum was home to 'Mrs Jack' Gardner herself, until her death in 1924. A monument to one woman's taste for acquiring exquisite art, the Gardner is filled with almost two thousand priceless objects, primarily European, including outstanding tapestries and Italian Renaissance and 17th-century Dutch paintings. The four-story greenhouse courtyard is a masterpiece and a tranquil oasis that alone is worth the price of admission.

⊙ Map p116, C4

www.gardnermuseum.org

280 The Fenway

adult/child/student/senior $15/free/5/12

⊘ 11am-5pm Wed-Mon, to 9pm Thu

Ⓣ Museum

Don't Miss

Europa by Titian

The centerpiece of the second-floor Titian Room, this erotic painting was one of Mrs Gardner's favorites. As the story goes, the Roman god Jupiter disguised himself as a gentle white bull to seduce the princess Europa. He succeeded, and their offspring was supposedly the founder of Europe.

John Singer Sargent

Mrs Jack was a patron of John Singer Sargent, who often used the *palazzo* as a studio. In the first-floor Spanish Cloister, the dramatic painting of a flamenco dancer, *El Jaleo,* is framed by a Moorish arch designed specifically for this space. Upstairs, the Gothic Room contains a stunning (and controversial) portrait that Sargent painted of his patron.

Tapestry Room

This great hall is hung with 10 enormous tapestries entitled *Scenes from the Life of Cyrus the Great* and *Scenes from the Life of Abraham.* Oddly, they are hung rather haphazardly – according to Mrs Gardner's whim – instead of sequentially.

Empty Frames

On March 18, 1990, two thieves disguised as police officers broke into the Gardner and left with nearly $200 million worth of artwork, including paintings by Vermeer, Rembrandt, Manet and Degas, not to mention French and Chinese artifacts. The crime was never solved, and the frames still hang empty, to honor Mrs Jack's request that her collection never be altered.

☑ Top Tips

▸ Admission to the Gardner is free on your birthday! If your name is Isabella, admission is free *every* day.

▸ Free tours and public talks are offered nearly every day, including an hour-long Collection Highlights Tour (at noon and 2pm on weekdays).

▸ Decked with ancient art and seasonal blooms, the courtyard is glorious from any angle. Check it out from the upper-story windows.

✕ Take a Break

If there is free table at the elegant **Café G** (mains $12-19; ⏱11am-4pm Wed-Mon, to 8pm Thu), you'll receive a pager so you can continue to explore the *palazzo* until your table is ready. Alternatively, exit the museum and stroll across the Back Bay Fens for a quick but satisfying lunch at **El Pelon** (p117).

Top Sights
Fenway Park

What is it that makes Fenway Park 'America's Most Beloved Ballpark'? It's not just that it's the home of the Boston Red Sox. Open since 1912, it's the oldest operating baseball park in the country. As such, the park has many quirks that make for a unique experience at Fenway Park. To learn the history and find out what's so special about Fenway Park, take the hour-long tour of this beloved Boston landmark. Bonus: see the ballpark from atop the Green Monster!

Map p116, C2

www.redsox.com

4 Yawkey Way

tours adult/child/senior $17/12/14

9am-5pm Apr-Oct

Kenmore

Red Sox game, Fenway Park

Don't Miss

Green Monster

As all Red Sox fans know, 'the wall giveth and the wall taketh away.' The 37ft-high left-field wall is only 310ft away from home plate (compared to the standard 325ft), so it's popular among right-handed hitters, who can score an easy home run with a high hit to left. However, a powerful line drive can bounce off the Monster for an off-the-wall double.

Scoreboard

At the base of the Green Monster is the original scoreboard, still updated manually from behind the wall.

Pesky Pole

The Pesky Pole, Fenway's right-field foul pole, is named for former shortstop Johnny Pesky. Johnny 'Mr Red Sox' Pesky was associated with the team for 60 years – 15 as a player and 45 as a coach or manager.

The Triangle

Many a double has turned into a triple when the ball has flown in the deepest, darkest corner of center field (where the walls form a triangle). At 425ft, it's the furthest distance from home plate.

Red Seat

The bleachers at Fenway Park are green, except for one lone red seat: seat 21 at section 42, row 37. This is supposedly the longest home run ever hit at Fenway Park – officially 502ft, hit by Red Sox left fielder Ted Williams in 1946.

☑ **Top Tips**

▶ Tours depart at the top of the hour. Buy tickets at the Gate D ticket booth.

▶ If you want to see a game, it's best to buy tickets (p119) well in advance. Game-day tickets go on sale (one per person) at Gate E, 90 minutes before the game, but people start lining up well before that.

▶ On game days, you can watch the teams warm up if you join a special 'batting practice tour' ($25).

✗ **Take a Break**

Concessions line the ballpark's breezeway, selling hotdogs, nachos, pretzels and beer. Outside the ballpark, you'll find food and drink at the **Bleacher Bar** (p118) or any of the joints along Landsdowne St.

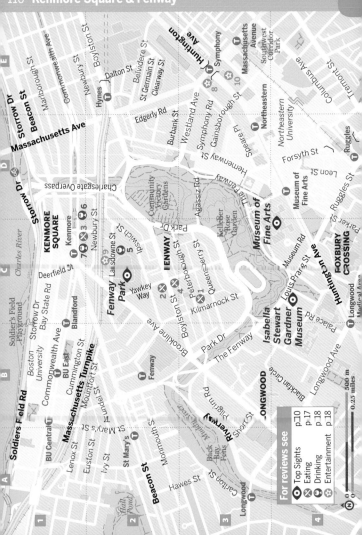

For reviews see
- Top Sights p10
- Eating p17
- Drinking p18
- Entertainment p18

500 m
0.25 miles

Tasty Burger

Eating

El Pelon
TAQUERIA $

1 Map p116, C3

Boston's best burritos, tacos and *tortas* (flat-bread sandwich), made with the freshest ingredients. The *tacos de la casa* are highly recommended, especially the *pescado,* made with Icelandic cod and topped with chili mayo. (www.elpelon.com; 92 Peterborough St; tacos $3-6; 11am-11pm; ; Museum)

Tasty Burger
BURGERS $

2 Map p116, C2

Once a gas station, now a retro burger joint, with picnic tables outside and a pool table inside. You won't find Kobe beef on your bun, but you will have to agree that it's a 'tasty burger.' (www.tastyburger.com; 1301 Boylston St; burgers $4-6; 11am-2am; ; Fenway)

Island Creek Oyster Bar
SEAFOOD $$$

3 Map p116, C1

Island Creek has united 'farmer, chef and diner in one space' – and what a space it is. ICOB serves up the region's finest oysters, along with other local seafood, in an ethereal, new-age setting. The specialty lobster-roe noodles (topped with braised short ribs and grilled lobster) lives up to the hype. (617-532-5300; www.islandcreekoysterbar. com; 500 Commonwealth Ave; oysters $2.50-

4, lunch mains $18-21, dinner mains $25-35; ⏱4pm-1am; T Kenmore)

Citizen Public House   AMERICAN $$

4 Map p116, C2

Long overdue on this side of Fenway Park, this is a modern, urban gastropub with food and drinks for a sophisticated palate. There's an eye-catching and daily-changing raw bar, while the list of main dishes focuses on roasts and grills. The food is top-notch and complemented by an extensive bar menu, featuring 75 varieties of whiskey – the Ideal Manhattan is an award-winner. (📞617-450-9000; www.citizenpub.com; 1310 Boylston St; mains $15-23; ⏱dinner daily, brunch Sun; T Fenway)

Drinking

Bleacher Bar   SPORTS BAR

5 Map p116, C2

Tucked under the bleachers at Fenway Park, this classy bar offers a view onto center field. Not the best place to watch the game, but it's an awesome way to experience America's oldest ballpark, even when the Sox aren't playing. (www.bleacherbarboston.com; 82a Lansdowne St; ⏱11am-1am Sun-Wed, to 2am Thu-Sat; T Kenmore)

Lower Depths Tap Room   BAR

6 Map p116, D1

A beer-lovers' paradise; besides the impressive beer selection, the kitchen turns out excellent comfort food, including one-dollar Fenway Franks with exotic toppings. Cash only. (www.thelowerdepths.com; 476 Commonwealth Ave; ⏱11:30am-1am; T Kenmore)

Hawthorne   COCKTAIL BAR

7 Map p116, C1

In the basement of the Hotel Commonwealth, this living room-style cocktail lounge attracts sophisticates. Sink into plush furniture and sip a cocktail. (www.thehawthornebar.com; 500a Commonwealth Ave; ⏱5pm-2am; T Kenmore)

Entertainment

Boston Symphony Orchestra   CLASSICAL MUSIC

8 ⭐ Map p116, E3

Near-perfect acoustics match the ambitious programs of the world-renowned orchestra. From September to April, the BSO performs in the beauteous Symphony Hall, featuring a high-relief ceiling and attracting a dressed-up crowd. The building was designed in

○ Local Life
Music in the 'Hood

Say a prayer of thanks for this neighborhood music venue. **Church** (Map p116, C3; www.churchofboston.com; 69 Kilmarnock St; cover $10-12; ⏱5pm-2am; T Museum or Kenmore) books cool bands nightly and has pool tables, a pretty slick restaurant and attractive people.

Understand
Citgo Sign

It's an unlikely landmark in this high-minded city, but Bostonians love the bright-blinking 'trimark' that has towered over Kenmore Sq since 1965. Every time the Red Sox hit a home run over the leftfield wall at Fenway Park, Citgo's colorful logo is seen by thousands of fans.It also symbolizes the end of the Boston Marathon, as it falls at mile 25 in the race.

Bostonians have claimed these lights as their own. When Citgo decided to dismantle the deteriorating sign in the 1980s, residents fought to bestow landmark status on the sign to preserve it. And the sign stayed. In 2005, the neon lights were replaced with LEDs (more durable, more energy-efficient and easier to maintain). Featured in film, photos and song, the sign continues to shine.

1861 with the help of a Harvard physicist who pledged to make the building acoustically perfect (he succeeded). (BSO; ☎617-266-1200; www.bso.org; Symphony Hall, 301 Massachusetts Ave; tickets $30-115; ⓣSymphony)

Fenway Park   SPORT
From April to September you can watch the Red Sox play at the nation's oldest and most storied ballpark (see ◉ Map p116, C2). It's also the most expensive – not that this stops the faithful from scooping up the tickets. There are sometimes game-day tickets on sale at Gate E, starting 90 minutes before opening pitch. (www.redsox.com; 4 Yawkey Way; tickets $26 125; ⓣKenmore)

House of Blues   LIVE MUSIC
9 ⭐ Map p116, C2

The HOB is bigger and better than ever. Well, it's bigger. This is where na-

tional acts play if they can't fill the Garden (such as the reunited J Geils Band, Lady Gaga, Dropkick Murphys). The balcony seating offers an excellent view of the stage, while fighting the crowds on the mezzanine can be brutal. (www.hob.com/boston; 15 Lansdowne St; ⓣKenmore)

Huntington Theatre Company   DRAMA THEATRE
10 ⭐ Map p116, E3

Boston's award-winning theater company, the Huntington specializes in developing new plays, staging many shows before they're transferred to Broadway (several of which have won Tony Awards). The company's credentials also include more than 50 world premieres of new works, by playwrights such as Tom Stoppard and Christopher Durang. (Boston University Theatre; www.huntingtontheatre.org; 264 Huntington Ave; ⓣSymphony)

Explore

Cambridge

Stretched out along the north shore of the Charles River, Cambridge is a separate city that boasts two distinguished universities, a host of historic sites, and artistic and cultural attractions galore. The streets around Harvard Sq are home to restaurants, bars and music clubs that rival their counterparts across the river.

The Sights in a Day

First things first: the star of Harvard Sq is – you guessed it – **Harvard University** (p122). Take a tour of the historic campus, then visit one of the university's top-notch museums, such as the **Peabody Museum of Archaeology & Ethnology** (p127) or the newly reopened **Harvard Art Museum** (p127).

Afterwards, have lunch at **Mr Bartley's Burger Cottage** (p129) or **Clover Food Lab** (p128). Spend the afternoon strolling along Tory Row, popping into the **Longfellow National Historic Site** (p128) and wandering around **Mt Auburn Cemetery** (p128).

When you next get hungry, head to **Cambridge, 1** (p128) or **Russell House Tavern** (p130) for dinner. In the evening, your options are nearly unlimited for cultural fare, whether it's live music, theater or film.

To see what locals love about Cambridge, check out Offbeat Harvard Square (p124).

⊙ Top Sights

Harvard Yard (p122)

◯ Local Life

Offbeat Harvard Square (p124)

 **Best of Boston**

Eating

Clover Food Lab (p128)

Cambridge, 1 (p128)

Mr Bartley's Burger Cottage (p129)

Drinking

Beat Hotel (p130)

Entertainment

American Repertory Theater (p131)

Comedy Studio (p131)

Sinclair (p132)

Regattabar (p132)

Museums

Harvard Art Museum (p127)

Peabody Museum of Archaeology & Ethnography (p127)

Harvard Museum of Natural History (p127)

Getting There

Ⓣ **Metro** Take the red line to Harvard or Central.

Top Sights
Harvard Yard

Founded in 1636 to educate men for the ministry, Harvard is America's oldest college. The original Ivy League school has eight graduates who went on to be US presidents, not to mention dozens of Nobel Laureates and Pulitzer Prize winners. The geographic heart of Harvard University – where red-brick buildings and leaf-covered paths exude academia – is Harvard Yard (through Johnston gate from Massachusetts Ave).

⊙ Map p126 D3

www.harvard.edu

Massachusetts Ave

tours free

⊙ tours hourly 10am-3pm Mon-Sat

T Harvard

Science Center, Harvard Yard

Don't Miss

Massachusetts Hall & Harvard Hall
Flanking Johnston Gate are the two oldest buildings on campus. South of the gate, Massachusetts Hall houses the offices of the President of the University. Dating to 1720, it is the oldest building at Harvard and the oldest academic building in the country. North is Harvard Hall, which dates to 1766 and originally housed the library.

John Harvard Statue
Every Harvard hopeful touches this statue's shiny shoe for good luck. Inscribed 'John Harvard, Founder of Harvard College, 1638,' the sculpture is known as the statue of three lies: it does not actually depict Harvard, but a random student; John Harvard was not the founder of the college, but its first benefactor; and the college was actually founded in 1636.

Widener Library
Behind this mass of Corinthian columns and steep stairs are more than 5 miles of books. Widener was built in memory of rare-book collector Harry Elkins Widener, who perished on the *Titanic*. Apparently Harry gave up his seat in a lifeboat to retrieve his favorite book from his stateroom. The library is not open to the public.

Memorial Hall
North of Harvard Yard, just outside Bradstreet Gates and across the Plaza, this massive Victorian Gothic building was built to honor Harvard's Civil War heroes. The impressive Memorial Transept is usually open for visitors to admire the stained-glass windows and stenciled walls. Most of the building's artistic treasures are contained in Annenburg Hall, which is not open to the public.

☑ Top Tips
▶ Free, student-led historical tours depart from the Smith Campus Center on an hourly basis from 10am to 3pm, Monday through Saturday (less frequently in winter).

▶ To go it alone, pick up a self-guided tour from the campus center or download an audio file or mobile app from the website.

▶ Finish your tour by climbing the steps of Robinson Hall for a perfectly framed photo of Memorial Hall.

✗ Take a Break
Harvard Square is packed with places to eat and drink, including several spots at the Smith Campus Center. You can't go wrong at **Clover Food Lab** (p128) or **Mr Bartley's Burger Cottage** (p129).

Local Life
Offbeat Harvard Square

Overflowing with coffee houses and pubs, bookstores and record stores, street musicians and sidewalk artists, panhandlers and professors, Harvard Sq exudes energy, creativity and nonconformity – and it's all packed into a handful of streets between the university and the river.

1 **The Pit**

Start your tour in the center of Harvard Sq, where **Out of Town News** (Harvard Sq; ⊙6am-9pm; **T**Harvard) has been selling newspapers and magazines from around the world since 1955. The sunken area nearby, aka 'the Pit,' is a popular spot for street artists, skateboarders and counterculture youth to congregate.

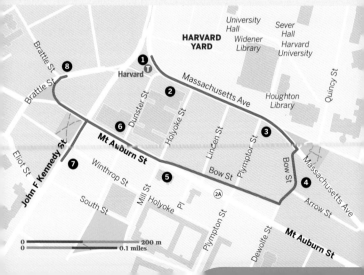

❷ Smith Campus Center

The sidewalk cafe in front of the main **administrative building** (www.harvard. edu/visitors; 1350 Massachusetts Ave; ⏱9am-5pm Mon-Sat) has hosted an ongoing chess tournament for 30 years and counting – look for the 'Play the Chessmaster' sign. It also offers a front-row seat to watch the buskers, beggars and other Harvard Sq hullabaloo.

❸ Harvard Bookstore

Family owned and operated since 1932, the **Harvard Bookstore** (www.harvard. com; 1256 Massachusetts Ave; ⏱9am-11pm Mon-Sat, 10am-10pm Sun) is not officially affiliated with the university, but it's the community's favorite place to browse, and hosts readings, lectures and author talks almost every weeknight. Next door, **Grolier Poetry Bookshop** (www.grolierpoetrybookshop. org; 6 Plympton St; ⏱11am-7pm Tue & Wed, to 6pm Thu-Sat) is the oldest and perhaps most famous poetry bookstore in the USA. Through the years, TS Eliot, ee cummings, Marianne Moore and Allen Ginsberg have all passed through.

❹ Café Pamplona

For sustenance, make your way to this hidden gem. This no-frills European **cafe** (12 Bow St; mains $8-15; ⏱11am-midnight) in a cozy backstreet cellar has been serving coffee and tea to Cantabrigian bohemians since 1959.

❺ In Your Ear

One of several excellent used record shops in the square, **IYE** (www.iye.com; 72 Mt Auburn St; ⏱11am-8pm Mon-Sat, noon-6pm Sun) is located in the basement of a Harvard social club. It's totally disorganized, dusty and crammed with LPs and 45s, as well as CDs, DVDs and even eight-tracks.

❻ The Garage

This gritty **mini-mall** (36 John F Kennedy St; ⏱10am-9pm) (yes, formerly a parking garage) houses an eclectic collection of offbeat shops. Try on sweet streetwear at Kulturez, listen to tunes at Newbury Comics, or get some ink at Chameleon Tattoo & Body Piercing.

❼ Raven Used Books

Tucked into a tiny basement, **Raven** (www.ravencambridge.com; 52 John F Kennedy St; ⏱10am-9pm Mon-Sat, 11am-8pm Sun) knows its audience: its 14,000 books focus on scholarly titles, especially in the liberal arts. This beloved shop is one of the last used-bookstore holdouts in Harvard Sq.

❽ Brattle Square

A few steps from the historic **Brattle Theatre** (www.brattlefilm.org; 40 Brattle St), this intersection is a main stage for street performers. Tracy Chapman played here in the 1980s and Amanda Palmer was a living statue here in the 1990s. Puppeteer Igor Fokin also put on shows here until his unexpected death in 1996. Look for the bronze memorial marionette, erected 'in celebration of all street performers.'

N 0 ___ 200 m
0 ___ 0.1 miles

For reviews see
⊙	Top Sights	p122
⊙	Sights	p127
⊗	Eating	p128
◐	Drinking	p130
☆	Entertainment	p131
🔒	Shopping	p132

Massachusetts Ave

Hauser Hall

Oxford St

Semitic Museum

Austin Hall

Law School

2 Harvard Museums of Science & Culture

Divinity Ave

Phillips Pl

Mason St

James St

HARVARD SQUARE

Cambridge Common

Science Center

Schlesinger Library

Radcliffe Yard

Dawes Island

Peabody St

Memorial Hall, Sanders Theater

Cambridge St

Old Burying Ground

3

14

Appian Way

11

Farwell Pl

18

Battle St

Church St

6

Harvard Hall

University Hall

Memorial Church

Broadway

Robinson Hall

Harvard Art Museum

1

Story St

15

Palmer St

12

Massachusetts Hall

Harvard Yard

Mt Auburn St

Mifflin Pl

7

10

17

Cambridge Visitor Information Kiosk

Carpenter Center

Quincy St

Brattle St

19

Dunster St

T Harvard

Widener Library

Prescott St

University Rd

Bennett St

Eliot St

Holyoke St

Linden St

5

8

13

Harvard St

16

Kennedy School of Government

Winthrop St

South St

Bow St

Mt Auburn St

Massachusetts Ave

Arrow St

John F Kennedy St

Mill St

Plympton St

Dewolfe St

Athens St

Grant St

Banks St

Copperwaite St

John F Kennedy Park

Weld Boathouse

Memorial Dr

Charles River Bike Path

Charles River

JEAN-PIERRE LESCOURRET/GETTY IMAGES ©

Lawn at Harvard University

Sights

Harvard Art Museum   MUSEUM

1 ◎ Map p126, D3

Architect extraordinaire Renzo Piano
has overseen a renovation and expansion of Harvard's art museum, allowing
the university's massive 250,000-piece
collection to come together under one
very stylish roof – with separate collections devoted to Asian and Islamic
cultures, Northern European and
Germanic cultures and other Western
art, especially European modernism.
It's slated to open by the end of 2014.
(www.harvardartmuseum.org; 32 Quincy St;
Ⓣ Harvard)

Harvard Museums of Science & Culture   MUSEUM

2 ◎ Map p126, D1

At the **Peabody Museum of Archaeology & Ethnology**, the impressive
exhibits examine indigenous cultures
throughout the Americas. Next door,
the esteemed **Harvard Museum of
Natural History** is famed for for its
botanical galleries, featuring more
than 3000 lifelike pieces of hand-
blown glass flowers and plants.
(www.hmsc.harvard.edu; 11 Divinity Ave;
adult/child/senior $12/8/10; ⊙9am-5pm;
🚌86, Ⓣ Harvard)

Longfellow House HISTORIC HOUSE

3 👁 Map p126, A2

Brattle St's most famous resident was Henry Wadsworth Longfellow, whose stately manor is now a National Historic Site. The poet lived and wrote here for 45 years, from 1837 to 1882, writing many of his most famous poems, including *Evangeline* and *The Song of Hiawatha*. Accessible by guided tour, the Georgian mansion contains many of Longfellow's belongings as well as lush period gardens. (www.nps.gov/long; 105 Brattle St; admission free; ⊙tours 9:30am-4:30pm Wed-Sun Jun-Oct, grounds dawn-dusk year-round; 🚍71 or 73, ⓉHarvard)

Mt Auburn Cemetery CEMETERY

4 👁 Map p126, A3

On a sunny day, this delightful spot at the end of Brattle St is worth the 30-minute walk west from Harvard

---

Understand
Tory Row

Heading west out of Harvard Square, **Brattle Street** is the epitome of colonial posh. Lined with mansions that were once home to royal sympathizers, the street earned the nickname Tory Row. Look for Longfellow House, once headquarters for George Washington and later home to the epic poet.

Sq. Developed in 1831, it was the first 'garden cemetery' in the US. Maps pinpoint the rare botanical specimens and notable burial plots. (www.mountauburn.org; 580 Mt Auburn St; admission free; ⊙8am-5pm Oct-Apr, to 7pm May-Sep; 🅿; 🚍71 or 73, ⓉHarvard)

Eating

Clover Food Lab VEGETARIAN $

5 🍴 Map p126, C4

Clover is on the cutting edge. It's all high-tech with its 'live' menu updates and electronic ordering system. But it's really about the food – local, seasonal, vegetarian food – which is cheap, delicious and fast. How fast? Check the menu. Interesting tidbit: Clover started as a food truck (and still has a few trucks making the rounds). (www.cloverfoodlab.com; 7 Holyoke St; mains $6-7; ⊙7am-midnight, Mon-Sat, to 7pm Sun; 🍴👶; ⓉHarvard)

Cambridge, 1 PIZZA $$

6 🍴 Map p126, B3

Set in the old fire station, this pizzeria's name comes from the sign chiseled into the stonework out front. The interior is sleek, sparse and industrial, with big windows overlooking the Old Burying Ground in the back. The menu is equally simple: pizza, soup, salad, dessert. These oddly-shaped pizzas are delectable,

Understand

Understand
Massachusetts Institute of Technology (MIT)

The MIT campus offers a novel perspective on Cambridge academia: proudly nerdy, but not quite as tweedy as Harvard, MIT seems to pride itself on being offbeat. Wander into a courtyard and you might find it graced with a sculpture by Henry Moore or Alexander Calder...or you might just as well find a ping-pong table or a trampoline. It's worth a wander to see what they'll come up with next.

Guided campus tours depart from the **information center** (www.mit. edu; 77 Massachusetts Ave; ⊙9am-5pm Mon-Fri; Ⓣ Central), and they also have a worthwhile **science museum** (museum.mit.edu; 265 Massachusetts Ave; adult/child $8.50/4; ⊙10am-5pm; Ⓟ[♿]; Ⓣ Central).

with crispy crusts and creative topping combos.
(www.cambridge1.us; 27 Church St; pizzas $17-22; ⊙11:30am-midnight; [✎]; Ⓣ Harvard)

Alden & Harlow
MODERN AMERICAN $$

7 Map p126, B3

This brand new place in a cozy subterranean space is offering a brand new take on American cooking. The small plates are made for sharing, so everyone in your party gets to sample – and you'll want to, because these local ingredients are prepared in ways you've never seen before. PS: It's no secret that the 'Secret Burger' is amazing.
([☎]617-864-2100; www.aldenharlow.com; 40 Brattle St; small plates $9-17; ⊙5pm-1am Sun-Wed, to 2am Thu-Sat; Ⓣ Harvard)

Mr Bartley's Burger Cottage
BURGERS $$

8 Map p126, C4

Packed with small tables and hungry college students, this burger joint has been a Harvard Square institution for more than 50 years. Bartley's offers at least 40 different burgers; if none of those suit your fancy, create your own 7oz juicy masterpiece with the toppings of your choice. Sweet-potato fries, onion rings, thick frappes and raspberry-lime rickeys complete the classic American meal.
(www.mrbartley.com; 1246 Massachusetts Ave; burgers $10-15; ⊙11am-9pm Mon-Sat; [♿]; Ⓣ Harvard)

Russell House Tavern

MODERN AMERICAN $$

9 Map p126, B3

Smack dab in the middle of Harvard Sq, this attractive gastropub has a classy, classic atmosphere, enhanced by good-looking, effervescent patrons. The menu – with hints of Southern goodness – includes a raw bar and a list of intriguing but irresistible small plates, not to mention a well-selected, all-American wine list and killer cocktails.

(www.russellhousecambridge.com; 14 John F Kennedy St; sandwiches & pizza $13, mains $19-26; ⏱11am-midnight, from 10am Sat & Sun; TⒽHarvard)

○ Local Life
Food Trucks

Food trucks cruise the city streets, serving up cheap, filling foods to those short on time and/or money – from ethnic eats to burgers and dogs, seafood, vegetarian, dessert and more.

Boston's food truck phenomenon started in Cambridge near MIT, where trucks catered to hungry students. They're still there, but you'll also find them near Harvard Yard, on the Boston Common, and on the Rose Kennedy Greenway. Our favorites include the following:

▶ **Roxy's Gourmet Grilled Cheese** (www.roxysgrilledcheese.com)

▶ **Clover Food Lab** (p128)

▶ **Chicken & Rice Guys** (www. cnrguys.com)

For more information, check out the **Boston Food Truck Blog** (http://bostonfoodtruck.wordpress. com).

Drinking

Beat Hotel

BAR

10 Map p126, B3

A great new addition to Harvard Square, this underground bistro packs in good-looking patrons for international food, classy cocktails and live jazz and blues. It's inspired by the Beat Generation writers – and named for a rundown Parisian motel where they hung out – but there's nothing down-and-out about this hot spot.

(www.beathotel.com; 13 Brattle St; ⏱4pm-midnight Mon-Wed, to 2am Thu-Fri, 10am-2am Sat, 10am-midnight Sun; TⒽHarvard)

La Burdick

CAFE

11 Map p126, A3

This boutique chocolatier doubles as a cafe, usually packed full of happy patrons drinking hot cocoa. Whether you choose dark, milk or white, it's sure to be some of the best chocolate you'll drink in your lifetime. There are only a handful of tables, so it's hard to score a seat when temperatures are chilly.

KIM GRANT/GETTY IMAGES ©

Performers at Club Passim

(www.burdickchocolate.com; 52D Brattle St; ⏰8am-9pm Sun-Thu, to 10pm Fri & Sat; Ⓣ Harvard)

Entertainment

Club Passim   FOLK MUSIC

12 ⭐ Map p126, B3

Folk music in Boston seems to be endangered outside of Irish bars, but the legendary Club Passim books such top-notch acts that it practically fills in the vacuum by itself. The colorful, intimate room is hidden off a side street in Harvard Sq. Patrons can order filling dinners from Veggie Planet, an incredibly good restaurant that shares the space. (📞617-492-7679; www.clubpassim.org; 47 Palmer St; tickets $15-30; Ⓣ Harvard)

Comedy Studio   COMEDY

13 ⭐ Map p126, D4

The 3rd floor of the Hong Kong noodle house contains a low-budget comedy house with a reputation for hosting cutting-edge acts. This is where talented future stars (eg Brian Kiley, who became a writer for Conan O'Brien) refine their racy material. Each night has a different theme; on Tuesday you can usually see a weird magic show. (www.thecomedystudio.com; 1238 Massachusetts Ave; admission $10-12; ⏰show 8pm Tue-Sun; Ⓣ Harvard)

American Repertory Theater   PERFORMING ARTS

14 ⭐ Map p126, A3

There isn't a bad seat in the house at Harvard University's Loeb Drama Theater, where the prestigious ART stages new plays and experimental interpretations of classics. Since 2008 Artistic Director Diane Paulus has encouraged a broad interpretation of 'theater,' staging interactive murder mysteries, readings of novels in their entirety and robot operas. (📞617-547-8300; www.amrep.org; 64 Brattle St; tickets $40-75; Ⓣ Harvard)

BOSTON GLOBE/GETTY IMAGES ©

Performer Jessie Ware at Sinclair

Regattabar   JAZZ

16 ⭐ Map p126, A4

Regattabar looks just like a conference room in a hotel – in this case, the Charles Hotel. They get big enough names (Virginia Rodrigues, Keb Mo) to transcend the mediocre space, though. With only 225 seats, you're guaranteed a good view, and the sound system is excellent. (📞617-395-7757; www.regattabarjazz.com; 1 Bennett St; tickets $15-35; T Harvard)

Shopping

Cardullo's Gourmet Shop   FOOD & DRINK

17 🔒 Map p126, B3

We've never seen so many goodies packed into such a small space. You'll find every sort of imported edible your heart desires, from caviar to chocolate. The excellent selection of New England products is a good source of souvenirs. (www.cardullos.com; 6 Brattle St; ⏰9am-9pm Mon-Sat, 10am-7pm Sun; T Harvard)

Sinclair   LIVE MUSIC

15 ⭐ Map p126, B3

A great new small venue to see and hear live music, with excellent acoustics; the mezzanine level lets you escape the crowds on the floor. The club attracts a good range of local and regional bands and DJs. Under the direction of Michael Schlow, the attached kitchen puts out some delicious and downright classy food. (www.sinclaircambridge.com; 52 Church St; tickets $15-18; ⏰11am-1am Tue-Sun, 5pm-1am Mon; T Harvard)

Cambridge Artists' Cooperative   HANDICRAFTS

18 🔒 Map p126, B3

Owned and operated by Cambridge artists, this three-floor gallery displays an ever-changing exhibit of their work. The pieces are crafty – hand-

Local Life
Shays Pub & Wine Bar

A charming basement-level bar, **Shays** (Map p126, B4; www.shayspub andwinebar.com; 58 John F Kennedy St; ⊙11am-1am Mon-Sat, noon-1am Sun; T Harvard) is a long-standing favorite among Harvard graduate students. Inside, it's a small wooden pub where you can sit on a stool and pretend to look thoughtful. Out front is a small brick patio full of sunners and smokers jockeying for a table and watching the sidewalk goings-on.

made jewelry, woven scarves, leather products and pottery. The craftspeople double as sales staff, so you may get to meet the creative force behind your souvenir. (www.cambridgeartistscoop.com; 59a Church St; 10am-6pm Mon-Sat, to 8pm Thu, noon-8pm Sun; T Harvard)

Curious George Store

CHILDREN'S BOOKS

19 🔒 Map p126, B3

Find your favorite story about that mischievous monkey, but there are also thousands of other books and toys to choose from. Authors Margret and HA Rey lived for more than 30 years on nearby Brattle St. (www.thecuriousgeorgestore.com; 1 John F Kennedy St; ⊙10am-6pm Sun-Wed, to 8pm Thu-Sat; T Harvard)

The Best of
Boston

Charles River sculling team
STEVE DUNWELL/GETTY IMAGES ©

Best Walks
Freedom Trail

🏃 The Walk

The best introduction to revolutionary Boston is the Freedom Trail, a red-brick path that winds its way past 16 sites that earned Boston its status as the 'cradle of American liberty.' The 2.4-mile trail follows the course of the conflict, from the Boston Common to Bunker Hill. But even though it's called the Freedom Trail, it covers much more than just revolutionary history – you'll find some of Boston's oldest landmarks, and sites where Boston prospered in the post-revolutionary period.

Start Boston Common; 🚇 Park St

Finish Bunker Hill Monument; 🚇 Community College

Length 2.4mi; 3 to 4 hours

🍴 Take a Break

Quincy Market (p68) food court has myriad options for a quick lunch and several full-service restaurants. History buffs can dine at **Union Oyster House** (p68), the oldest restaurant in the US.

RICHARD CUMMINS/GETTY IMAGES ©

Freedom Trail marker

❶ Boston Common

The Freedom Trail starts at the **Boston Common** (p46), America's oldest public park. The 50-acre green is criss-crossed with walking paths and dotted with monuments. Don't miss the powerful monument to the victims of the Boston Massacre, erected in 1888.

❷ Massachusetts State House

Overlooking the Boston Common from the northeast corner, the **Massachusetts State House** (p52) occupies a proud spot atop the city's last remaining hill – land that was previously part of John Hancock's cow pasture. Other Sons of Liberty also had their hands in building the new capitol: Samuel Adams and Paul Revere laid the cornerstones on July 4, 1795.

❸ Park St Church

At the corner of the Common, the soaring spire of **Park Street Church** has been an unmistakable landmark since 1809. The church earned the moniker 'Brimstone Corner' for its usage as a gunpowder storage place (during the War of 1812) and for its fiery preaching.

❹ Granary Burying Ground

Heading north on Tremont St, you will pass the Egyptian Revival gates of the **Granary Burying Ground** (p52). Steeped in history, the serene cemetery is the final resting place of many of the Sons of Liberty, as well as the victims of the Boston Massacre and other historical figures.

❺ King's Chapel & Burying Ground

Continue north to School St, where the Georgian **King's Chapel** (p65) overlooks its adjacent burying ground. It is perhaps an odd choice for inclusion on the Freedom Trail, since it was founded as an Anglican Church in 1688. It does contain a large bell crafted by Paul Revere, and the prestigious Governor's pew, once occupied by George Washington.

❻ Site of the First Public School

Turn east on School St, and take note of the bronze statue of Benjamin Franklin outside Old City Hall. A plaque commemorates this spot as the site

of the country's first public school. Enter the courtyard to discover some of the school's distinguished alumni and some quirky artwork.

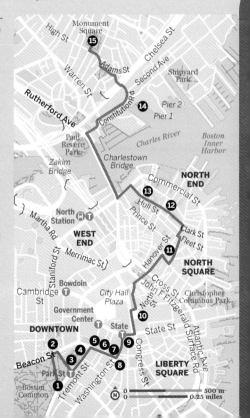

❼ Old Corner Bookstore

Continue to Washington St, where the little brick building is known as the Old Corner Bookstore, a literary and intellectual hotspot for 75 years. Strangely, now it is an option for lunch if you're in the mood for some Mexican fast food.

❽ Old South Meeting House

Across Washington St, the **Old South Meeting House** (p64) saw the beginnings of one of the American Revolution's most vociferous protests, the Boston Tea Party. Come off the street and listen to an audio re-enactment of what went down that day.

❾ Old State House

Before the revolution, the seat of the Massachusetts government was the **Old State House** (p64). Dodge the traffic to inspect the cobblestone circle that marks the site of the Boston Massacre, the revolution's first violent conflict in 1770;

gaze up at the balcony, where the Declaration of Independence was first read to Bostonians in 1776.

❿ Faneuil Hall

Historic **Faneuil Hall** (p65) was the city's original market and public meeting place, built in 1740. Admire the bronze statue of Samuel Adams, who sits astride his horse in Dock Square. Then ascend to the 2nd-floor hall, where Adams was one of many orators to speak out against the British rule.

⓫ Paul Revere House

Cross the Rose Kennedy Greenway and head into the heart of the North End. You will find yourself in charming North Sq. The weathered clapboard **Paul Revere House** (p50) is the oldest example in Boston, as most other wooden constructions were destroyed by fires. This is likely where Paul Revere commenced his famous midnight ride.

⓬ Old North Church

Back on Hanover St, walk two blocks north to Paul Revere Mall. Besides a dramatic statue of the patriot himself, this park also provides a lovely vantage point to view your next destination, the **Old North Church** (p36). In addition to playing a crucial revolutionary role, the 1723 church is also Boston's oldest house of worship.

⓭ Copp's Hill Burying Ground

From the church head west on Hull St to **Copp's Hill Burying Ground** (p37). This quiet corner contains some of the city's oldest gravestones and offers grand views across the river to Charlestown. See if you can find the headstone of Daniel Malcolm, which is littered with bullet holes from British troops, who apparently took offense at his epitaph.

Paul Revere House

⓮ USS Constitution

Walk across the bridge and continue to the **Charlestown Navy Yard** (p24), home of the world's oldest commissioned warship, the USS *Constitution*. Board the ship for a tour of the upper decks, where you will learn about her exploits in America's earliest naval battles.

⓯ Bunker Hill Monument

Walk through the winding cobblestone streets up to the 220ft granite obelisk that is the **Bunker Hill Monument** (p27). Check out the dioramas in the museum to better understand what transpired on that fateful day in June 1775. Then climb 294 steps to the top of the monument to enjoy the panorama of the city, the harbor and the North Shore.

Best Walks
Green Spaces & Shopping Places

🏃 The Walk

Everybody knows about the world-class museums and historical sites, but Boston also offers a network of verdant parks, welcoming waterways and delightful shopping streets, making it a wonderful walking city. Take a break from the crowded downtown streets and discover another side of Boston.

Start Boston Common; T Park St

Finish Boston Common; T Park St

Length 2.5mi; 3 hours

🍴 Take a Break

Fuel up with a coffee and pastries from **Wired Puppy** (p104) on Newbury St or **Flour** (p101) near Copley Sq. If you've worked up an appetite by the end of the walk, grab a meal at **Paramount** (p53).

Lagoon, Public Garden

BARRY WINIKER/GETTY IMAGES ©

❶ Boston Common

Welcome to the country's **oldest public park** (p46), sprinkled with monuments and memorabilia. Follow busy Bostonians crisscrossing the Common and exit the park from the western side.

❷ Public Garden

The **Public Garden** (p52) is a 24-acre botanical oasis of Victorian flowerbeds, verdant grass and weeping willows shading a tranquil lagoon. Don't miss the famous statue *Make Way for Ducklings*, based on the beloved children's book.

❸ Newbury Street

Exiting the Garden through the southwestern gate, stroll west on swanky **Newbury St** (p96) for some window-shopping and people-watching.

❹ Copley Square

Boston's most exquisite architecture centers on this stately Back Bay plaza. The Romanesque **Trinity Church** (p94) is particularly lovely as reflected in the modern

John Hancock Tower. Opposite, the elegant neo-Renaissance **Boston Public Library** (p92) is packed with treasures.

❺ Commonwealth Avenue

Heading north, cross stately Commonwealth Ave, the grandest of the Back Bay's grand avenues. Lined with brownstones and studded with 19th-century art, the 'Mall' offers an eclectic perspective on history.

❻ Charles River Esplanade

The southern bank of the Charles River Basin is known as the **Esplanade** (p104) – an enticing urban escape with grassy knolls and cooling waterways designed by Frederick Law Olmsted. Walk east, enjoying the breezes and views of the river.

❼ Charles Street

Intriguing history, iconic architecture and unparalleled neighborhood charm makes Beacon Hill one of Boston's most

prestigious addresses. Traversing the flat of the hill, **Charles St** (p55) is an enchanting spot for browsing boutiques and haggling over antiques.

❽ Louisburg Square

Stroll down residential streets lit with gas lanterns; admire the distinguished brick town houses decked with flower boxes; and discover streets like stately **Louisburg Sq** (p53) that capture the neighborhood's grandeur. Continue south to return to the Common.

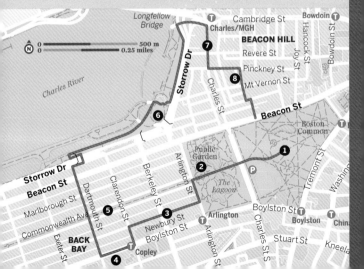

Best
Eating

The Boston area is the home of the first Thanksgiving and of bountiful autumnal harvests. It's also America's seafood capital, the origin of dishes such as clam chowder and boiled lobster (p69). This regional cuisine has deep cultural roots – and like all things cultural, is dynamic and continuously developing.

TRAVEL PIX LTD/GETTY IMAGES ©

International Influences

The international influence on Boston cuisine cannot be underestimated. Italian, Irish and Portuguese are already old-hat; now Bostonians are sampling Brazilian, Chinese, Indian, Korean, Thai and Vietnamese. Immigrants open restaurants to cater to their own community, but these exotic eateries are also attracting the attention of well-traveled Bostonians who are curious about global cultures.

Farm to Table

In this era of creative culinary discovery, more and more Bostonians are reclaiming their roots in one crucial way: their appreciation of local, seasonal and organic products. A thriving 'locavore' movement highlights the bounty from the local waters and from rich New England farms.

Vegetarians & Vegans

The **Boston Vegetarian Society** (www.bostonveg.org) is a great resource for vegetarian eaters, with extensive restaurant reviews and lots of links to veggie-friendly organizations. It also organizes a fabulous two-day food festival in October.

☑ **Top Tips**

▶ In restaurants with table service, leave a 15% tip for acceptable service and a 20% tip for good service – any less shows dissatisfaction with your waiter. Waitstaff and bartenders are paid significantly below minimum wage and depend on tips for their earnings.

Best Location

Courtyard Inside the beautiful Boston Public Library. (p100)

Sam's at Louis On the waterfront, with expansive views of Boston Harbor. (p67)

Bistro du Midi Overlooks the Public Garden. (p101)

Best Budget Eating

El Pelon Cheap and delicious tacos galore. (p117)

Clover Food Lab From the food truck or from the restaurant. (p128)

Galleria Umberto Lunch for less than $5. (p39)

Best Seafood

Neptune Oyster Casual but classy, with a well-stocked raw bar. (p39)

Yankee Lobster Co A retail fish market serving the freshest fish around. (p67)

Row 34 A dozen types of mollusks are served at this 'working man's oyster bar.' (p67)

Atlantic Fish Co All kinds of seafood, any way you like it. (p103)

Island Creek Oyster Bar Eat your seafood in style. (p117)

Best Italian

Pomodoro The quintessential romantic North End hideaway, with great food. (p39)

Giacomo's Ristorante Old-fashioned food and old-fashioned prices. (p39)

Grotto An inviting underground restaurant serving innovative takes on Italian. (p53)

Coppa An authentic *enoteca* experience. (p82)

Best Chinese

Gourmet Dumpling House Ridiculously good soup dumplings in a no-nonsense setting. (p82)

Winsor Dim Sum Cafe An itty-bitty restaurant with top-notch dim sum. (p84)

Myers & Chang A hip South End spot serving pan-Asian delights. (p82)

Best Pizza

Pizzeria Regina The queen of pizza in Boston. (p40)

Cambridge, 1 Oddly shaped, thin-crust pizza with interesting, innovative toppings. (p128)

Picco Carefully crafted pizzas and homemade ice cream. (p83)

Best Vegetarian

Clover Food Lab Fast food, made fresh, with no animals involved. (p128)

Veggie Planet Pizza and stir-fries set to a folk-music soundtrack. (p131)

My Thai Vegan Café Veggie versions of many meat dishes. (p84)

Best Bakeries

Flour Perfection in a scone. (p140)

Maria's Pastry Maria Merola knows her cannoli. (p32)

Best Local Favorites

Casa Razdora Homemade pasta to go. (p67)

Sam La Grassa's Gigantic sandwiches keep the workers satisfied. (p67)

Falafel King Divey but delicious. (p67)

Trident Bookseller Sandwiches and salads, served with a side of good books. (p106)

Best
Drinking

Despite the city's Puritan roots, modern-day Bostonians like to get their drink on. While the city has more than its fair share of Irish pubs, it also has a dynamic craft-beer movement, with a few homegrown microbreweries; a knowledge-able population of wine drinkers; and a red-hot cocktail scene, thanks to some talented local bartenders. So pick your poison...and drink up!

JOHN COLETTI/GETTY IMAGES ©

☑ **Top Tips**

▶ Expect to pay a cover charge of $10 to $20.

▶ Most clubs enforce a dress code at the door.

▶ Go online to get on the guest list or re-serve a table to avoid being turned away at the door.

Where to Drink

Boston's drinking scene is dominated by four cat-egories: dive bars, Irish bars, sports bars and a new breed of truly hip cocktail bar. Any of these types might cater to discerning beer drinkers, with local craft brews on tap or a wide selection of im-ported bottles. Some also morph into dance clubs as the night wears on.

If you prefer caffeine to alcohol, there are scores of cute cafes and cool coffeehouses, many of which serve dynamite sandwiches and pastries. Many offer wireless internet (sometimes for a fee), which is basically an invitation to stay all day.

Where to Dance

There's really only one neighborhood in Boston for dancing: the Theater District. Boylston St is the main drag for over-the-top megaclubs, but there are other venues all over this groovy 'hood, and a few classier clubs in Back Bay, Cambridge and Downtown.

Best Views

Top of the Hub The view from the top of the Pru is fine indeed. (p104)

Pier Six Head to Charlestown for a spectacular panorama of the city skyline. (p29)

Bleacher Bar Sneak a peek inside Fenway Park. (p118)

Maria's Pastry (p32)

Best Vibe

Beehive A modern-day speakeasy with music, food and drink. (p84)

Beat Hotel Creativity pervades this jazz-music brasserie. (p130)

Best for Beer

Tip Tap Room A truly excellent selection of craft beers on tap. (p54)

Harpoon Brewery Free samples on the brewery tour. (p70)

Best for Cocktails

Drink Unparalleled for mixology madness. (p68)

Ward 8 A newcomer named after Boston's original cocktail. (p41)

Best for Coffee

Thinking Cup Treat yourself to a frothy hazelnut latte. (p68)

Best Sports Bars

Bleacher Bar The ultimate baseball bar. (p118)

Caffé dello Sport Join the locals sipping Campari and watching football. (p42)

Best for GLBT

Club Café Tasty food, friendly people, good times. (p85)

Fritz The only gay sports bar in town – a South End original. (p84)

Best Nightclubs

Good Life Get your groove on here. (p70)

Underbar Best. Sound system. Ever. (p85)

Best Local Favorites

Zume's Coffee House Where the Townies go for coffee. (p29)

Caffé Paradiso Do the North End thing. (p42)

21st Amendment A Beacon Hill hangout for pols and their staffers. (p54)

Lucky's Lounge Every day is Throwback Thursday at Lucky's. (p70)

Delux Café Experience the South End before gentrification. (p85)

Best
Entertainment

Welcome to the Athens of America, a city rich with artistic and cultural offerings. With the world-class Boston Symphony Orchestra and several nationally ranked music schools, Boston is a musical mecca. The Theater District is packed with venues showcasing the city's opera, dance and dramatic prowess, while more innovative experimental theaters are in Cambridge and the South End.

LOU JONES/GETTY IMAGES ©

Best for High Culture

Boston Symphony Orchestra The city's pride and joy. (p118)

Opera House Home of the Boston Ballet. (p70)

Cutler Majestic Theatre Home of Opera Boston. (p86)

Best for Rock

Sinclair Great small venue for new bands. (p132)

Church Local bands perform every night. (p118)

House of Blues Where the big names play. (p119)

Best for Jazz & Blues

Red Room @ Cafe 939 Cool place with up-and-coming acts. (p105)

Regattabar Great jazz in an intimate setting. (p132)

Best for Drama

American Repertory Theater Cutting-edge theater in Cambridge. (p131)

Huntington Theatre Company Boston's biggest and best-known company. (p119)

Boston Center for the Arts Multipurpose space used by dozens of small companies. (p79)

☑ Top Tips

▶ **BosTix** (www.bostix. org; ⏱10am-6pm Tue-Sat, 11am-4pm Sun) has several locations offering discounted tickets to theater productions citywide.

▶ The BSO (p118) offers various discounted ticket schemes for classical music on the cheap.

Best for Comedy

Wilbur Theatre Boston's premier comedy club. (p87)

Improv Asylum Spontaneous fun in basement digs. (p42)

Comedy Studio Low-budget, cutting-edge funny stuff. (p131)

Best
Shopping

Boston is known for its intellect and its arts, so you can bet it's good for bookstores, art galleries and music shops. These days, the streets are also sprinkled with offbeat boutiques, some carrying vintage treasures and local designers. Besides to-die-for duds, indie shops hawk handmade jewelry, exotic household decorations and arty, quirky gifts. It's fun to browse, even if you don't intend to buy.

FRANZ MARC FREI/GETTY IMAGES ©

☑ **Top Tip**

▶ There's no sales tax in Massachusetts on clothing purchases up to $175.

Best for Local

South End Open Market A weekly extravaganza of arts and crafts. (p88)

Cambridge Artists' Cooperative Artist-owned and -operated. (p132)

NOA Beautiful stuff, locally made. (p54)

Best Women's Fashion

Crush Boutique Sweet clothes and on-point fashion advice. (p55)

Twilight Dress up for a night out on the town. (p43)

Lunarik Fashions Handbags in every shape, size and color. (p97)

Best Men's Fashion

Bobby from Boston Primo selection of new and vintage duds. (p88)

Sault New England A small but stylish boutique. (p88)

Ball & Buck Good-looking gear for manly men. (p97)

Best for Boston Souvenirs

Lucy's League Look good and support the team. (p71)

Sault New England Carefully curated New England stuff. (p88)

Blackstone's of Beacon Hill Quirky, clever gifts with a Boston theme. (p54)

Beacon Hill Chocolates Something for your sweet tooth. (p55)

Best Independent Bookstores

Harvard Bookstore Still in the square, still independent. (p125)

Trident Booksellers Good books, good coffee, good food. (p106)

Brattle Book Shop Lose an afternoon in this antiquarian bookstore. (p71)

Raven Used Books A basement crammed with books you want. (p125)

Best
For Kids

Boston is one giant history museum, the setting for many educational and lively field trips. Cobblestone streets and costume-clad tour guides can bring to life the events your kids have read about in history books. Hands-on experimentation and interactive exhibits fuse education and entertainment.

Sights & Activities

There are loads of museums and activities geared to kids, but even adult-oriented sites (such as art museums) have special programs to engage younger guests. Most museums and activities are free for children aged two years and under, with reduced rates for kids under 13 years. The Museum of Fine Arts (p110) is free for kids after 3pm on weekdays and all day on weekends. The Institute of Contemporary Art (p60) is always free for kids age 17 years and under.

Sleeping & Eating

Families are a prime target market for the tourist industry in Boston, so most hotels, restaurants and tour services will do their best to accommodate your kids. Hotels often invite children to stay free in the room of their paying parent. Also, look for children's menus and high chairs in most restaurants, and changing stations in public facilities.

WALTER BIBIKOW/GETTY IMAGES ©

☑ Top Tips

▶ Kids under age 12 ride the T for free.

▶ For more ideas, check out *Kidding Around Boston* by Helen Byers.

Best Kid Museums

New England Aquarium
Explore the most exotic of natural environments: under the sea. (p58)

Boston Children's Museum Hours of fun climbing, constructing and creating. Especially good for kids aged three to eight. (p66)

Museum of Science
More opportunities to combine fun and learning than anywhere in the city. (p36)

Skating on the Frog Pond (p48)

Harvard Museum of Natural History Almost as good as the zoo, with room after room of stuffed animals. (p127)

Best Adventures

Boston Harbor Islands Family-friendly facilities (and beach) on Spectacle Island. (p73)

New England Aquarium Whale Watch Whale sightings are practically guaranteed. (p66)

Best Tours for Kids

Duck Boats Kids of all ages can drive the boat on the Charles River. Bonus: quacking is encouraged. (p154)

Boston by Foot Offers the only child-centered tour of the Freedom Trail. (p154)

Urban AdvenTours Rents kids' bikes, helmets and trailers. (p37)

Best Parks & Playgrounds

Boston Common Contains a huge playscape with swings, jungle gyms and all the rest. (p46)

Public Garden Swan boats on the lagoon are perfect for little tykes. (p52)

Charles River Esplanade The Stoneman Playground is a picturesque riverside playground with separate areas for different ages. (p104)

Best Cool Stuff

Prudential Center Skywalk Observatory The view from above. (p100)

Mapparium The view from inside the earth. (p100)

Best Eating for Kids

Quincy Market This big food court will satisfy the pickiest palate. (p68)

Pizzeria Regina Classic pizza in the heart of the North End. (p40)

Mr Bartley's Burger Cottage Good old-fashioned burgers with all (or none) of the toppings. (p129)

City Landing Upscale dining for families. (p68)

Best
Museums

Don't get a rainy day get you down – Boston is packed with world-class museums that will keep you entertained and educated...and dry.

IVANASTAR/GETTY IMAGES ©

Something Different

Redefining what it means to be a 'museum', **Design Museum Boston** (http://designmuseumboston.org) brings the goods to you. This 'pop-up' museum launches temporary exhibits in public spaces all around town, from shopping malls to public parks to airports. Keep your eyes open – design is all around you.

Best Art Museums

Museum of Fine Arts Boston's premier venue for art spanning the centuries and the globe. (p110)

Institute of Contemporary Art Sometimes spectacular and sometimes strange, but always stimulating. (p60)

Isabella Stewart Gardner Museum An exquisite Venetian *palazzo* packed with art. (p112)

Harvard Art Museum Three museums under one fabulous new roof. (p127)

Best Science Museums

New England Aquarium All the creatures of the sea, on full display. (p58)

Museum of Science Hundreds of exhibits and experiments to thrill your inner scientist. (p36)

Harvard Museum of Natural History Glass flowers, stuffed animals and more. (p127)

MIT Museum From holograms to robots, explore how the world of science works. (p129)

Best History Museums

Boston Tea Party Ships & Museum An interactive museum that allows visitors to participate in revolutionary events. (p64)

Old State House Authentic artifacts and interesting exhibits, especially focusing on the Boston Massacre. (p64)

USS Constitution Museum Learn all about a sailor's life in 1812 and the history of the US Navy. (p25)

Museum of Afro-American History Rotating exhibits highlighting Boston's African-American history. (p52)

Best
Spectator Sports

Boston is fanatical about sports. And why not, with four professional sports teams – the Bruins, Celtics, Patriots and Red Sox – all piling up championships in recent years?

Baseball

In 2004, the Boston Red Sox broke an agonizing 86-year losing streak and won the World Series, repeating the feat in 2007 and in 2013. The Red Sox play from April to September at Fenway Park (p119), the nation's oldest and most storied ball park.

Basketball

The Boston Celtics have won more championships than any other NBA team, most recently in 2008. From October to April, they play at TD Garden (p42).

Football

Super Bowl champions in 2002, 2004 and 2005 (that's a 'three-peat'

for football fans), the **New England Patriots** (www.patriots.com) play at Gillette Stadium, 32 miles south of Boston in Foxborough. The season runs from late August to late December.

Ice Hockey

Stanley Cup winners in 2011, the Boston Bruins play ice hockey at TD Garden (p42) from mid-October to mid-April. College hockey is also huge, as Harvard, Boston College and Boston University teams earn the devotion of spirited fans.

Best Annual Sporting Events

Boston Marathon (www. baa.org; ☺3rd Mon Apr) One of the country's

most prestigious marathons takes place on Patriot's Day.

Head of the Charles Regatta (www.hocr. org) Spectators line the Charles River in mid-October to watch the world's largest rowing event.

Beanpot Tournament (www.beanpothockey.com) Rivalries come out in full force when local college hockey teams compete at this annual event in February.

Hub on Wheels (www. bostoncyclingcelebration. com) In September, this citywide bicycle ride starts at City Hall Plaza and offers three scenic routes of varying lengths.

Best
For Free

EDUCATION IMAGES/UIG/GETTY IMAGES ©

Boston can be an expensive city, but it only takes a bit of research to entertain yourself for free. Here are some options for culture vultures and history buffs with empty pockets. If you're hungry or thirsty, we've got a little something for you, too.

Free Tours

Freedom Trail NPS rangers lead free tours, departing from Faneuil Hall. (p154)

Black Heritage Trail Free walking tour, free history lesson. (p52)

Harvard University Free student-led historical tours. (p122)

Free Art & History

Boston Public Library Free internet access, free guided tours, free books (but you have to give them back). (p92)

Massachusetts State House Free admission, free tours. (p52)

Charlestown Navy Yard Free tour of the USS *Constitution*. (p24)

Bunker Hill Monument Free view from the top (but you have to climb up there). (p27)

Free Parks & Gardens

Public Garden Stop and smell the roses. (p52)

Rose Kennedy Greenway Frolic in fountains and walk the labyrinth for free. (p64)

Mt Auburn Cemetery Free garden walks, artistic headstones and views from Washington Tower. (p128)

Charles River Esplanade Free riverside strolling. (p104)

Free Museums

Institute of Contemporary Art Free admission every Thursday after 5pm. Free admission for families on the last Saturday of the month. (p60)

Boston Children's Museum Almost-free admission ($1) on Friday nights after 5pm. (p66)

Free Eating & Drinking

Falafel King Free falafel! (p67)

Harpoon Brewery You'll pay for the tour but tastings are free. (p70)

Free Entertainment

Charles River Esplanade Free summer concerts at the Hatch Shell. (p104)

Shakespeare on the Common Free outdoor theater, picnic not included. (p49)

Harvard Square Free music by buskers; quality not guaranteed. (p124)

Best History

For all intents and purposes, Boston is the oldest city in America – and you can hardly walk a step over her cobblestone streets without stumbling over some historic site.

MARTIN KREUZER/GETTY IMAGES ©

Presidential Sites

The legacy of John F Kennedy is ubiquitous in Boston, but the official memorial to the 35th president is the **John F Kennedy Presidential Library & Museum** (www.jfklibrary. org; Columbia Point; adult/child/senior & student $12/9/10; ⏱9am-5pm; P; T JFK/UMass then free shuttle), a fitting tribute to his life and legacy.

In the suburb of Brookline, the **John F Kennedy National Historic Site** (www.nps.gov/jofi; 83 Beals St; admission free; ⏱9:30am-5pm Wed-Sun May-Oct; T Coolidge Corner) occupies the modest house that was JFK's birthplace and boyhood home. Matriarch Rose Kennedy's narrative sheds light on the family's life.

Best Historic Tours

Freedom Trail The city's best revolutionary sites. (p154)

Black Heritage Trail Learn about Boston's abolitionist movement. (p52)

Best Historic Pubs & Restaurants

Warren Tavern George Washington drank here. (p29)

Union Oyster House JFK was a regular, back in the day. (p68)

Last Hurrah The classic bar at the Omni Parker House evokes Old Boston. (p70)

Best Freedom Trail Sites

Old State House Interpreting the genesis of the American Revolution. (p64)

Granary Burying Ground Final resting place for patriots and rebels. (p52)

Massachusetts State House The original Hub of the Universe. (p52)

Bunker Hill Monument Climb to the top for the 360-degree view. (p27)

Best Gravesites

John Winthrop, King's Chapel Burying Ground First Governor of the Massachusetts Bay Colony. (p65)

Paul Revere, Granary Burying Ground The fearless rider and patriot. (p52)

Henry Wadsworth Longfellow, Mt Auburn Cemetery The poet who retold American history. (p128)

Best
Tours

Best Walking Tours

Freedom Trail Foundation (www.thefreedomtrail.org;) This educational nonprofit group breaks up the Freedom Trail into bite-size portions (eg Boston Common to Faneuil Hall, North End, etc). Tour guides are in period costume.

Boston by Foot (www.bostonbyfoot.com; adult/child $12/8; ⚫) This fantastic nonprofit offers 90-minute walking tours with specialty themes, including a kid-friendly version of the Freedom Trail.

Best Trolley Tours

Beantown Trolley (☎800-343-1328, 781-986-6100; www.brushhilltours.com; adult/child/senior $35/15/33; ⏱9:30am-4:30pm) The only trolley that offers service to the Museum of Fine Arts and the Seaport District. The price includes hotel

pickup and a harbor cruise.

Old Town Trolley (www.historictours.com; Long Wharf; adult/child/senior $36/17/33; ⚫; T Aquarium) The price includes free admission to the Old State House and a harbor cruise.

Upper Deck Trolley (www.bostonsupertours.com; adult/child/senior $33/22/30; ⚫; T Aquarium) Super-tall trolleys give passengers a view over the traffic. This is the only trolley tour that goes to Cambridge. The two-day ticket also includes admission to a few museums.

Best Boat Tours

Duck Tours (☎617-267-3825; www.bostonducktours.com; adult/child/senior $35/24/29; ⚫; T Aquarium, Science Park or Prudential) These ridiculously popular tours use WWII amphibious vehicles that cruise the downtown

NEIL SETCHFIELD/GETTY IMAGES ©

streets before splashing into the Charles River. Tours depart from the Museum of Science or from behind the Prudential Center.

Codzilla (www.bostonharborcruises.com; 1 Long Wharf; adult/senior/child $27/23/25; ⏱10am, noon, 2pm & 4pm May-Sep, plus 3pm, 5pm & 6pm Jul & Aug; ⚫; T Aquarium) This 'tour' takes place on a 2800HP speedboat that cruises through the waves at high speeds. Painted like a multi-colored shark with a big toothy grin, the boat has a unique hull design that enables it to do the ocean version of doughnuts. You *will* get wet.

Survival Guide

Survival Guide

Before You Go

When to Go

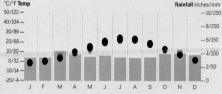

°C/°F **Temp**
50/122 —
40/104 —
30/86 —
20/68 —
10/50 —
0/32 —
-10/14 —
-20/-4 —

Rainfall inches/mm
— 10/250
— 8/200
— 6/150
— 4/100
— 2/50
— 0

J F M A M J J A S O N D

➡ **Spring (Apr–May)**
Mild weather accompanied by blooming magnolias and lilacs. Historic reenactments and marathon madness on Patriot's Day.

➡ **Summer (Jun–Aug)**
Hot and humid; locals make for the beach. Fireworks and fun on Independence Day.

➡ **Fall (Sep–Nov)** Cool crisp air and colorful leaves. Streets are once again filled with students.

➡ **Winter (Dec–Mar)**
Cold and snow-covered. The season comes festively with Christmas activities, but lasts too long.

Book Your Stay

Useful Websites

Boston Green Tourism (www.bostongreentourism. org) Up-to-date listings of green hotels.

Boston Luxury Hotels (www.bostonluxuryhotels. com) Offers individualized service for upscale travelers.

University Hotels (www. universityhotels.net) Find accommodations near a particular university.

Lonely Planet (www. lonelyplanet.com) Includes reviews and booking service.

Best Budget

HI Boston (www.boston hostel.org) A slick, new, state-of-the-art green facility with an excellent line-up of activities.

Friend Street Hostel
(www.friendstreethostel.
com) A friendly hostel on
Friend St.

Best Midrange

Oasis Guest House
(www.oasisgh.com) A
homey guesthouse in the
midst of the city.

Harborside Inn (www.
harborsideinnboston.com) A
renovated warehouse on
the waterfront.

Irving House (www.
irvinghouse.com) A gra-
cious, welcoming inn on a
residential street behind
Harvard Yard.

Best Top End

Inn @ St Botolph (www.
innatstbotolph.com) A
delightful brownstone
boutique emphasizing
affordable luxury.

Newbury Guest House
(www.newburyguesthouse.
com) Interconnected
town houses in a prime
location.

Liberty Hotel (www.
libertyhotel.com) Formerly
the notorious Charles
Street Jail, now a luxuri-
ous five-star hotel.

Arriving in Boston

☑ **Top Tip** For the best
way to get to your accom-
modation, see p17.

From Logan International Airport

➡ Silver line 'rapid' bus to
South Station, with a free
transfer to the T.

➡ Blue line T to central
Boston; take the free
shuttle from the airport
to the Airport T station.

➡ Water shuttle to the
Boston waterfront; take
the free shuttle to the
ferry dock.

➡ Taxi $15–25

From Manchester Airport

➡ Located one hour north
of Boston.

➡ Shuttle service pro-
vided by **Flightline, Inc**
(www.flightline.com).

From TF Green Airport

➡ Located one hour south
of Boston.

➡ MBTA commuter rail
to Back Bay or South
Station.

From South Station

➡ Red-line T station in
central Boston.

Getting Around

Bicycle (Hubway)

☑ **Best for...** short trips
around town.

➡ **New Balance Hubway**
(www.thehubway.com; 30min
free, 60/90/120min $2/6/14;
⏱24hr) is a bike-share
program that offers bikes
for short-term loan.

➡ Purchase a temporary
membership at any
bicycle kiosk, then pay by
the half hour for the use
of the bikes (free under
30 minutes). Return the
bike to any station in the
vicinity of your destina-
tion.

➡ There are 140 Hubway
stations around town;
check the website for
locations.

Boat

☑ **Best for...** scenic
rides on the water, including trips to the Boston

Harbor Islands and to Charlestown.

➡ The MBTA runs the **F4 ferry** (Map p26, D3; www.mbta.com; $1.70; ⏰6:30am-8:30pm Mon-Fri, 10am-6:30pm Sat-Sun; Ⓣ Aquarium) between Pier 3 in Charlestown and Long Wharf.

➡ **Boston Harbor Cruises** (www.boston harborcruises.com; 1 Long Wharf; Ⓣ Aquarium) offers seasonal ferry service (adult/child $15/9) from Long Wharf to the Boston Harbor Islands.

➡ **City Water Taxi** (www. citywatertaxi.com; Long Wharf; ⏰7am-10pm Mon-Sat, to 8pm Sun) makes runs from Long Wharf to the airport and other waterside destinations.

Bus
☑ **Best for...** outlying areas, including the airport.

➡ The **MBTA** (☎617-222-5215; www.mbta.com) operates bus routes, with schedules posted on its website and at some bus stops along the routes.

➡ The standard bus fare is $1.50, or $1.25 with a plastic 'Charlie Card'. If you're transferring from

the T with a Charlie Card the bus fare is free.

➡ The silver line, a so-called 'rapid' bus, services the airport (SL1). The fare is $2 ($1.70 with a Charlie Card).

Metro (The T)
☑ **Best for...** almost anywhere that is too far to walk.

➡ The **MBTA metro** (☎800-392-6100, 617-222-3200; www.mbta.com; per ride $2-2.50; ⏰5:30am-12:30am Sun-Thu, to 2am Fri & Sat) is known locally as the 'T'. There are four lines – red, blue, green and orange – radiating from the principal downtown stations.

➡ Buy a paper fare card ($2 per ride) or a Charlie Card ($1.70 per ride) at any station. (Request a Charlie Card from the attendant before adding value at the machine.)

➡ Tourist passes with unlimited travel (on subway, bus or water shuttle) are available for one week ($15) or one day ($9), at select stations.

➡ Kids under 12 ride free.

➡ The T operates approximately from 5:30am to 12:30am Sunday to Thursday, and to 2am Friday and Saturday nights.

Taxi
☑ **Best for...** rainy days and late nights.

➡ Cabs are plentiful but expensive. Rates are determined by the meter, which calculates miles.

➡ Expect to pay about $12 to $18 between most tourist points within the city limits, without much traffic.

Essential Information

Electricity

120V/60Hz

120V/60Hz

Emergency

➡ **Ambulance/police/ fire** (☏911)

Money

➡ **Automatic Teller Machines** ATMs are ubiquitous but most of them charge a fee (at least $2) if your account is with a different bank.

➡ **Changing Money** Change foreign currency for US dollars at Logan International Airport.

➡ **Credit Cards** Credit cards – especially Visa and MasterCard – are accepted at most hotels, restaurants, gas stations, shops and car-rental agencies.

➡ **Tipping** Many members of the service industry depend on tips to earn a living. Be sure to tip baggage handlers ($2 per bag), servers and bartenders (20% for good service), housekeeping ($5 for a weekend) and taxi drivers (10% to 15%).

Public Holidays

New Year's Day January 1

Martin Luther King Jr's Birthday Third Monday in January

Presidents' Day Third Monday in February

Evacuation Day March 17

Patriot's Day Third Monday in April

Memorial Day Last Monday in May

Independence Day July 4

Labor Day First Monday in September

Columbus Day Second Monday in October

Veterans Day November 11

Thanksgiving Day Fourth Thursday in November

Christmas Day December 25

Dos & Don'ts

➡ Do stay to the right on busy sidewalks, bike paths and subway escalators.

➡ Don't compare Boston to New York: it's irrelevant.

➡ Do chat with locals about baseball, politics or anything!

➡ Don't mimic or mock the local accent. And don't 'pahk yah cah in Hahvahd Yahd' – you'll get a ticket.

Telephone

☑ **Top Tip** All US phone numbers consist of a three-digit area code followed by a seven-digit local number. Always dial ☏1 + all 10 digits.

Phone Codes

Area codes Boston & Cambridge ☏617; Suburban Boston ☏781; North Shore ☏978; South Shore ☏508

Country code ☏1 for USA

International dialing code ☏011

160 Survival Guide

Cell Phones

➔ Most US cell-phone systems are incompatible with the GSM 900/1800 standard used throughout Europe and Asia.

Tourist Information

Boston Common Information Kiosk (GBCVB Visitors Center; www.boston usa.com; ⏲8:30am-5pm) Starting point for the Freedom Trail and many other walking tours.

Boston Harbor Islands Pavilion (www.bostonharbor islands.org; Rose Kennedy Greenway; ⏲9am-6pm May-Oct; Ⓣ Aquarium) Conveniently located on the Rose Kennedy Greenway.

Cambridge Visitor Information Kiosk (www. cambridge-usa.org; Harvard Sq; ⏲9am-5pm Mon-Fri, 1-5pm Sat & Sun; Ⓣ Harvard) Detailed information on current Cambridge happenings and self-guided walking tours.

National Park Service Visitors Center (NPS Faneuil Hall; www.nps.gov/bost; Faneuil Hall; ⏲9am-6pm; Ⓣ State) A new NPS facility in Faneuil Hall, with information about the Freedom Trail sights.

Travelers with Disabilities

Boston tries to cater to those with disabilities by providing cut curbs, accessible restrooms and ramps on public buildings, but old streets, sidewalks and buildings mean that facilities are not always up to snuff.

Sights Most major museums are accessible to wheelchairs, while several museums offer special programs and tours for travelers with disabilities.

Activities Many tours use vehicles that are wheelchair accessible. Walking tours are also accessible, though the historic buildings may not be.

Transportation MBTA buses are accessible, although not all subway trains and stations are. See **MBTA Accessibility** (www.mbta.com/accessibility) for more information. Ferries to the Boston Harbor Islands are all accessible.

Visas

Getting into the United States can be a bureaucratic nightmare, depending on your country of origin. To make matters worse, the rules are rapidly changing. For up-to-date information about visas and immigration, check with the **US State Department** (www.unitedstatesvisas.gov).

Visa Waiver Program

The Visa Waiver Program allows citizens of certain countries to enter the US (for stays of up to 90 days) without a visa. This list of eligible countries is subject to continual re-examination. Under this program you must have:

➔ A round-trip or onward ticket that is nonrefundable in the US.

➔ A machine-readable passport from an eligible country.

➔ A passport valid for at least six months longer than your intended stay.

Electronic Authorization

The **Electronic System for Travel Authorization** (ESTA; www.esta.us) is a pre-authorization system that is *mandatory* to use for the Visa Waiver Program.

➔ Register with ESTA online as soon as possible, and at least 72 hours prior to departure. It costs $4 to apply, and a further $10 when an application is approved.

➡ Once approved, registration is valid for two years, but you will need to re-register if you renew your passport or change your name.

Visa Applications

If you need to apply for a visa, you may be required to submit any or all of the following:

➡ A recent photo (50.8mm x 50.8mm).

➡ Documents of financial stability and/or guarantees from a US resident (particularly for travelers from developing countries).

➡ Visa applicants may be required to 'demonstrate binding obligations' that ensure their return home.

➡ Your passport should be valid for at least six months longer than your intended stay.

➡ The validity period for a US visitor visa depends on your home country. The actual length of time you'll be allowed to stay in the US is determined by the Bureau of Citizenship and Immigration Services at the port of entry.

Behind the Scenes

Send Us Your Feedback

We love to hear from travelers – your comments help make our books better. We read every word, and we guarantee that your feedback goes straight to the authors. Visit **lonelyplanet.com/contact** to submit your updates and suggestions.

Note: We may edit, reproduce and incorporate your comments in Lonely Planet products such as guidebooks, websites and digital products, so let us know if you don't want your comments reproduced or your name acknowledged. For a copy of our privacy policy visit lonelyplanet.com/privacy.

Mara's Thanks

Thanks to my two monkeys for accompanying me on many adventures, and for encouraging me to slow down and rediscover these places that I have visited so many times before. (Thanks to Jerry, Carrie and Elsida that I didn't have to take those monkeys on every adventure.)

Acknowledgments

Cover photograph: Sailing boats near the Charles River Esplanade (p104), Massimo Borchi/4Corners.

This Book

This 2nd edition of Lonely Planet's *Pocket Boston* was researched and written by Mara Vorhees, who also wrote the 1st edition. It was produced by the following:

Destination Editor Dora Whitaker **Product Editor** Kate James **Senior Cartographer** Mark Griffiths **Book Designer** Wendy Wright **Assisting Editors** Ali Lemer, Tracy Whitmey **Cover Research** Naomi Parker **Thanks to** Martine Power, Alison Ridgway, Dianne Schallmeiner, Angela Tinson, Juan Winata

Index

See also separate subindexes for:

⊗ **Eating p165**

🄳 **Drinking p166**

✪ **Entertainment p166**

🄰 **Shopping p167**

Sights p000
Map Pages **p000**

😋 Eating

A

Alden & Harlow 129
Atlantic Fish Co 103

B

Barking Crab 67-8
Bistro du Midi 101
Butcher Shop 83

C

Café G 113
Café Pamplona 125
Cambridge, 1 128-9
Carmelina's 39-40
Carmen 40
Casa Razdora 67
Citizen Public
House 118
City Landing 68
Clover Food Lab 47, 128
Coppa 82
Courtyard 100

E

Earl of Sandwich 47
El Pelon 117

F

Falafel King 67
Figs 28
Flour 101

G

Galleria Umberto 39
Gallows 79
Giacomo's
Ristorante 39
Gigi Gelateria 33
Gourmet Dumpling
House 82
Grotto 53

Our Writer

Mara Vorhees

Born and raised in St Clair Shores, Michigan, Mara traveled the world (if not the universe) before finally settling in the Hub. She spent several years pushing papers and tapping keys at Harvard University, but she has since embraced the life of a full-time travel writer, covering destinations as diverse as Russia and Belize. She lives in a pink house in Somerville, Massachusetts with her husband, two kiddies and two kitties. She is often seen eating doughnuts in Union Sq and pedaling her bike along the Charles River. The pen-wielding traveler is the author of Lonely Planet's *Boston* city guide and *New England*, among other titles. Follow her adventures online at www.havetwinswilltravel.com.

Published by Lonely Planet Publications Pty Ltd
ABN 36 005 607 983
2nd edition – Dec 2014
ISBN 978 1 74179 926 2
© Lonely Planet 2014 Photographs © as indicated 2014
10 9 8 7 6 5 4 3 2 1
Printed in China.